SQUEEZE YOUR HOME FOR CASH

101

Great Money Making Ideas for Homeowners

Ruth Rejnis

Real Estate
Education Company
a division of Dearborn Financial Publishing, Inc.

While a great deal of care has been taken to provide accurate and current information, the ideas, suggestions, general principles and conclusions presented in this text are subject to local, state and federal laws and regulations, court cases and any revisions of same. The reader is thus urged to consult legal counsel regarding any points of law—this publication should not be used as a substitute for competent legal advice.

Publisher: Anita A. Constant
Editor-in-Chief: Caroline Carney
Acquisitions Editor: Christine E. Litavsky
Managing Editor: Jack L. Kiburz
Editorial Assistant: Stephanie C. Schmidt
Interior Design: Lucy Jenkins
Cover Design: S. Laird Jenkins Corporation

Published by Real Estate Education Company,
a division of Dearborn Financial Publishing, Inc.

Printed in the United States of America

95 96 97 10 9 8 7 6 5 4 3 2 1

Library of Congress Cataloging-in-Publication Data

Rejnis, Ruth
    Squeeze your home for cash : 101 great money-making ideas for
homeowners / by Ruth Rejnis.
        p.   cm.
    Includes index.
    ISBN 0-7931-0991-4 (pbk.)
    1. Finance, Personal.   2. Real estate investment   I. Title
HG179.R393   1995   94-33694
332.024—dc20   CIP

ACKNOWLEDGMENT

A sincere thank you to the homeowners who so generously shared their experiences and tips for the readers of this book.

CONTENTS

PART III
Paperwork

INTRODUCTION

Do you always seem to be a little short of cash? Do you have too much month left at the end of your money?

Before you head out to find a second job or hit the automatic teller machine for yet another cash advance, stop right where you are—at home—and think. You have poured a great deal of cash into your place—in down payment, mortgage payments, maintenance and improvements. Now it's time to *make* some money. In fact, it's time to squeeze your house dry.

Many homeowners are unaware of how many money-making, and money-saving opportunities their homes offer, but there are plenty—certainly 101. Each is spelled out in the pages that follow, from quick tips that can put a little more change in your pocket to more detailed suggestions that can bring you thousands of dollars of extra income each year.

While not everyone will be able to take advantage of every single suggestion (or, will want to, for that matter), dozens are workable for all homeowners, from the single mom living in a Cape Cod, to the retirees at their beach house, to the extended family in a brownstone, to the new graduate in his or her condominium.

By squeezing your home for as much cash as it will yield, you may soon see your debts drop, the quality of your life improve and more money turn up in your hands.

You will have taken control and turned your home from the money pit they all seem to be to a superb *money-maker*. Congratulations. You're living, in good part, "on the house"!

PART ONE

Digging for Dollars

CHAPTER 1

Remodeling?
You Can Save While
Spending

Renovation. Restoration. Rehab. Remodeling. The need for fixing up a home never ends; nor, it seems, does the desire to have the latest in design and architectural features. Many homeowners find themselves always doing something around their place.

If you are thinking about spending several thousand dollars on the project *you* have in mind, can you still manage to save some money?

You sure can!

What's Involved Here

While selling your home might be a few years down the road, it is important to keep that day in mind *now*, as you plan a remodeling project. Naturally, you will want to make the greatest profit possible. Some improvements will help you do that (more about them later), while others will not impress buyers at all.

Another point worth mentioning in these early pages is local zoning regulations. It would be wise to see if you *can* make the improvement you want before giving it another moment's thought.

The Cardinal Rule

In home remodeling, it is: Don't overimprove.

William Young, director of consumer affairs for the National Association of Home Builders, says, "You want to consider what the improvement you want to make will do to the cost of your house in relation to others in the neighborhood.

"If you're living in a neighborhood where all of the homes cost $150,000, and you put in an expensive swimming pool that puts your house over that figure, chances are you're not going to be able to recover that pool cost," Young explains. "You can't consider your home in a vacuum, and say, 'Well, I spent $20,000 for this, I'll get $17,000 back.'"

That is by far the most important caution to home remodelers. But you might consider this, too: Your home is, of course, your castle. If you want to build an in-ground pool, go ahead and do it. However, it would be wiser to build it only if you are planning to stay in that house several more years, so it repays you in enjoyment if not in dollars from your cash investment.

Young explains how builders deal with specialization. "When you're designing for a subdivision," he says, "you don't want to put in features that make the house so unique or different that people won't want to buy it."

The Best Remodeling Projects

Fads and trends come and go. But some home improvements remain in style, such as the following:

- An upgraded kitchen. According to the National Kitchen and Bath Association, the average kitchen renovation costs $20,000. Are *you* mulling over a rehab? Good for resale, but it could put a real squeeze on your budget. Perhaps a cosmetic makeover will bring the effect you want at a far lower cost. You can have new paint or wallpaper, new flooring and countertops and, instead of costly new cabinets, have the existing ones refinished or the doors replaced. If the appliances are in good working order, you can spray paint them to match the new color scheme, instead of buying new ones.
- A remodeled bath. Here again, while you *can* buy everything new—fixtures, flooring, tile—there is money to be saved by tak-

ing it easy here, if the fixtures are all right. A built-in vanity around the sink, for example, can cover ugly pipes and provide extra storage space. So can new shelving on the walls. Add fresh paint or wallpaper, and inexpensive flooring or carpeting instead of a higher-priced tile. Have the tub reglazed at a cost of around $200, and you can boast an attractive, better-functioning bath for far less than the cost of a full-scale remodeling.

- An added bathroom. The one-bathroom house is often sniffed at in these days of two, two-and-a-half and even three full baths in new homes. Adding an extra bath to a one-bedroom house is likely to at least pay back its cost at resale time, and help the house sell faster. Are there any money-saving angles? Fitting the bath into an existing space in the house, especially if that is near plumbing lines, will cost less than having to add on the room.
- A master suite. An area that has become very popular over the last few years, this consists of a bedroom, a dressing room (or two) and perhaps his-and-hers baths. Can you save on such a seemingly large-scale project? Here is another instance where you can if you are able to carve out the space from existing rooms, instead of having to build new ones.
- A sun space/sun room. Usually, but not always, added on to the kitchen or dining area, this space brings the outdoors inside, but without the discomfort: heat, humidity, bugs, rain, etc. Your utility company can offer advice on cooling and heating, so you can use this new area all year round, at maximum energy savings.
- An attractive entryway. Yes, you never do get a second chance to make a first impression. Good-looking landscaping (along with a clean, freshly painted front of the house) can pay you back when you sell, and perhaps make the house move faster. There is more about landscaping choices in Chapter 5.
- A deck. Leisure areas are in, and so are outdoor decks, from simple layouts to sophisticated multilevel spaces. Here is an instance where your desires and buyers' preferences happily coincide. Money savings? Perhaps this is a job you can do yourself. But read on. One homeowner says, "*Yourself?* You're kidding."
- A finished attic In a continuing search for space, many homeowners look to the attic for an extra bedroom, home office or hobby space. A conversion can be inexpensive as long as the

existing stairway to the attic does not require walking through someone's bedroom, or there are more than pull-down steps. Insulation can be a concern, too.

- A skylight or two. Illuminating dark areas in the house—a hall-way or a windowless bathroom—can be a relatively inexpensive improvement (around $1,000 if you have a professional do the installing) that will improve the look of your home and pay you back its cost at resale.
- An exterior paint job. A solid expenditure, whether one is staying put for years or painting with the intention of selling. There is money to be saved if you do the job yourself. But watch out for cheap paint and brushes. Good quality *does* make a difference in the finished product, and top-grade paint and brushes are not that expensive. If you paint at or close to the color your house is now, you might be able to save by skipping a second coat.
- Replaced windows. Increasingly popular as we all look at the cost of wasted energy, this project can improve the appearance of your home, and save on utility bills, but don't expect to recoup the total expense here when you sell. Buyers will expect good windows.

The Do-It-Yourselfer

Should you hire out a remodeling job, or tackle it yourself? This is a difficult one to call, but here is a brief quiz that can help you decide. Be honest.

- Do you feel comfortable handling the improvement you want, based on past successes with smaller jobs around your home? William Young of the National Association of Home Builders says: "If you have no experience with any kind of construction activity, you can't simply pick up a book and say, 'I'm going to remodel the kitchen.' You learn from your mistakes. Unfortunately, your mistakes here can cost you money."
- Do you have a decent selection of tools? Not only will you need them, but what you have is also a good indication of your interest in, and ability to handle, repairs and upgrades around the house.
- Do you have time for this?

- Can you call in help if you need it? That means can you afford to turn the job over to a professional, and *will* you? Or can some buddies come over to help out? Some jobs become more involved than you would have thought. When Carol and Joe Jensen decided to build a deck themselves, they ended up calling on their grown son and a few of his friends to help out. "This isn't a job for one person, or even a couple," says Joe Jensen. "You need three people working together." That wood is *heavy*. Unwieldy, too.
- Deep down, do you *really* want to do it? If you don't, it will probably show in the work, and certainly in how long it will take you to complete the job.

Doing Some of It Yourself

If you don't think you can do it yourself, but still need to save money, here's a compromise: Let the contractor do the major stuff, while you do the finishing work. Or you do the hefty building, but farm out some specialized jobs.

Doug Tarencz built a 1,500-square-foot addition to his New Jersey home, increasing its size by one-third (no, that did not make the house larger than its neighbors). He did most of the work himself, but he hired out: laying the concrete garage floor, putting on a new roof and installing a skylight. He had premixed cement delivered.

He also hired an experienced helper who was looking to become a contractor to work with him for the duration of the project, which took about two years working part-time. Tarencz paid him an hourly rate.

"I figure I saved at least $50,000 by doing so much myself," Tarencz says. "Other than the jobs I flatly decided to hire out, my philosophy was I would try it and if I couldn't do it, I would hire somebody. There are very few things, aside from masonry work, that can't be taken apart and then done again."

When Chelle Delaney and her husband, George Carlson, bought a home in a southern city's historic district, they found there was much to do even though the house was not, strictly speaking, a fixer-upper.

"There was no built-in closet in one of the bedrooms," Delaney recalls. "And the kitchen had an old porcelain sink and no cabinets."

The couple took the "coach" route to affordable remodeling. Delaney took a course on historic preservation, "and we ended up hiring the guy who taught it. I worked side by side with him so I could see how he was doing the bathroom renovation." She learned how to put in new tiles and wallpaper and restore old woodwork and floors.

The couple also saved money doing "grunt" work themselves before the contractor or specialist came in. They predrilled and hammered in nails and picked up materials from suppliers and home centers to save time and money. They tore down walls, too, when that was needed.

"We didn't see any point in paying somebody to tear things up," Delaney explained. "Besides, that was exhilarating."

Hiring a Contractor

Perhaps you have decided by now to engage a contractor for your project. How do you find a satisfactory, even great, one?

Keep in mind that the better business bureau says the hiring of contractors is one of the two or three most common areas where they receive complaints. For your own protection, you had better do some homework before signing any checks.

The best way to find a jewel is, of course, through word of mouth. If you have neighbors who have had work done, ask them who their contractor was, if they were pleased with his work, and if you can take a look. You can even ask strangers, if you are driving by a house with remodeling underway. They may be happy to talk with you—especially if they are having major problems with the individual or company they have hired!

Interview several contractors. Get at least three bids for all the work needed. Check references the contractors give you, although this is rarely helpful. What contractor is going to give you the name of someone who was displeased? Call your local better business bureau and local or state department of consumer affairs to see if they have had any complaints about whomever you are considering.

When having a contractor over to give you an estimate, be sure he or she is clear about exactly what work you want done. You cannot compare bids if everyone is told something different about the project you are considering.

The bid that is *substantially* lower than the others is not the one to select. Sometimes those individuals operate without insurance, skimp on work or have other flaws. Usually the middle bid is the best deal.

The contractor to be wary of

- has no license to show you;
- has no proof of insurance;
- has no letterhead (acceptable for an individual who does odd jobs, but not for a contracting company);
- offers no print-contract, only a verbal agreement (get *everything* in writing);
- says you do not need a permit for certain work, when you know you do;
- advertises in the Yellow Pages and on panel trucks and shows only a telephone number, no address (Tarencz adds his own rating system here. He eliminated from consideration those who arrived for estimates in trucks that looked as if they had just pulled out of a swamp. If the contractor had a spanking new truck, with all the bells and whistles, Tarencz recalls, "I'd say to myself, "'That guy's going to be $2,000 above everybody else,' and that's what happened."); and
- asks for a large down payment up front. (One-third up front is common, with another third as work progresses and the final third on *satisfactory* completion of the job. If you can get by with 10 percent up front, go with that.)

The American Homeowners Foundation, a nonprofit education and research organization, offers a model contract you can use for a home improvement project. Send a check or money order for $6.95 to the foundation at 6776 Little Falls Rd., Arlington, VA 22213.

Do's, Don'ts and Points To Ponder

- If you are selling your home, it's wise to make only cosmetic changes, such as new interior and exterior paint and new carpeting. Let the new owners upgrade the kitchen.
- Always look to existing space that can be converted—a porch that can be enclosed, for example—before deciding to build. Have you been thinking about turning the attached garage into living quarters for an elderly parent or parent-in-law moving in? Sounds good, but the loss of a garage can work against you at resale time (although creating a studio apartment above a detached garage can be a plus, if local zoning laws allow).

- If you are adding a room to your home, traffic flow is important. Architects and builders say they often see rooms with poorly designed layouts (or those that seem not to have been designed at all), where you must walk through Billy's bedroom to get to Grandma's room. That kind of mishmash sends would-be buyers looking elsewhere.
- Building *up* is likely to be less costly than building *out*. With the former, plumbing and other mechanical systems need only be extended, not installed.
- You need a plan for some small remodeling projects. An inexpensive aid: See if you can engage an architect or interior designer to spend a half day or so at your place, at a flat per diem rate, or an hourly fee. You might end up paying as little as $100, certainly worth it if you are about to spend a few thousand.
- Reconsider "built-in" improvements, such as bookcases, stereo systems and the like. They cost more than freestanding units; they limit your flexibility when you want to redecorate; the next buyer might find them a drawback; and they can inflate your property taxes, since they are likely to be assessed as part of your home.
- If you are hiring a painter for the exterior of your house, ask him or her for references that include homes painted *several years ago*. New ones will always look fresh. It is the older jobs where poor painting will surface, in cracking, peeling and the like.
- Enter contests! Really. Kitchen and bath contests are held often by decorating magazines and some specialty groups. You can't get much cheaper than a *free* room. To help you along, write for the free booklet "Tips from the Experts: How to Enter Kitchen & Bath Remodeling Contests." Write USG Corporation, Department 147-4, PO Box 806278, Chicago, IL 60680.
- Don't forget your local utility company if you are making energy-saving improvements. It can give you printed material, and can also send over a representative to help explain where savings lie with certain products and installations. Maybe yours has a low-interest loan program, too, for certain projects.
- Remember to contact your insurance agent if you are doing a major remodeling. You will want to make sure your homeowners policy will keep up with that project.

- Hold on to all your remodeling receipts for tax breaks in the future, not just on next year's return. In fact, it is wise to keep them indefinitely.

How To Pay for It All

Chapter 20 talks about your options for a home improvement loan. You will be pleased to see you have quite a few choices, some at very favorable terms indeed.

Reading Material

Do not enter a major remodeling job without a plan. For ideas, read decorating and remodeling magazines and cut out pictures of rooms or improvements that you especially like. *Remodeling* magazine publishes regular surveys on cost versus value for a number of common home improvements, to give you an idea on the return you can expect, if any, with your project. There are also many books in the Home section of bookstores on remodeling and doing it yourself.

"Selecting a Professional Remodeling Contractor" is a free booklet, available by sending a self-addressed stamped envelope (SASE) to the National Association of the Remodeling Industry, Suite 310, 4301 N. Fairfax Dr., Arlington, VA 22203.

For another SASE you can receive the free booklet "How to Choose a Remodeler" from the National Association of Home Builders, Remodelers Council, 15th and M Sts., NW, Washington, DC 20005.

If you are interested in a kitchen rehab, you can write the National Kitchen and Bath Association (NKBA) for a list of their certified designers in your area. Those are people with the initials CKD (Certified Kitchen Designer) after their names. Write the NKBA at 687 Willow Grove St., Hackettstown, NJ 07840.

SUMMING UP

$ Don't overimprove your house for the neighborhood.

$ Keep in mind how any improvement is likely to affect the sale of your home, even if you are not thinking now about moving.

$ Know yourself: whether you can, and should, do the remodeling job, or whether you should hire it out.

$ Home contracting is an area rife with fraud. Do your homework before choosing someone to work on your house.

CHAPTER 2

How a Civic or Block Association Can Increase the Value of Your Home

The idea is simple: block residents, or neighbors in a larger residential area, working together to do whatever is best for that small community of homeowners.

You may have seen examples of this let's-pull-together spirit in your own town, especially in revival areas where homes—and neighborhoods—are brought back from a long slide toward blight. Their saviors are concerned groups of newcomers who join forces with the hardy residents who have remained, and together they achieve outstanding successes.

Perhaps such organizations have been operating for years where you live and hold respected positions in your city or town. They might be genuine historic districts or smaller, less recognized groups that are no less proud of the homes they represent.

A principal tenet of all organized groups of homeowners, however small, is the same: getting results. If John Doe wants a stop sign at the corner of Broad and Elm streets, he may well get the sign, but after much time and energy spent wending his way through the city hall maze. But, if the *Elm Street Block Association* wants a stop sign—well, you get the picture. The council member representing that district will treat the group's request as the most urgent of priorities because there are dozens, perhaps hundreds, of *votes* there.

That's the strength of these organizations. What are the financial benefits of uniting? How can these groups help you make money?

Besides strength in numbers when it comes to larger issues, the block or civic association spends time improving the appearance of members' homes and area streets. Window boxes appear at many houses thanks to a member's trip to a nursery to buy flowers at bulk rates. Trees are planted because someone in the organization tracked down free plantings from an office of city government. And when existing trees need trimming another member calls city hall to request that service, and keeps calling until it is satisfactorily completed.

Organized homeowners, concerned about the appearance of their neighborhood, can increase property values of homes within the association boundaries and also make houses there easier to sell. Because of all that attention and hard work, residents make their homes desirable. Desirable homes bring good prices to homesellers, who can get more for their houses than they could have in the old days of no organization and perhaps neighborhood disintegration. It is not unheard of in blocks or whole neighborhoods run tightly and well, for price wars to begin when a house goes on the market. Wouldn't you like *that* kind of attention for your place!

Community associations working to improve schools within their borders also greatly improve the value of those houses, since good schools are right at the top of many househunters' list of musts. It is not unheard of for home shoppers to buy for the *school* rather than an individual property.

Besides tending homes, these groups also provide an active social program for residents, which is another inducement to buyers since the group provides a ready source of socializing and making new friends.

If you are already in one of these associations, by all means read on. You might find some new projects for your group.

If you look around your neighborhood, and see that you all have a common bond—your homes were built by the same developer 70 years ago, for example, or all ring the city's largest park, or are all lakefront cabins, or are in a downtown area struggling for renewal—then form a civic association. Give yourselves a name and present a united force to the powers that be on the local, regional and even state level.

What's Involved Here

First, a few words of definition.

These groups are not to be confused with homeowners' associations that are often found in new-home communities of single-family or mixed-use developments, and are always found in condominium developments. Those associations require owners to join, and obey the community's bylaws. Membership is not optional; you must join as a condition of buying a home there.

These are the communities you read about where someone is being sued for painting his home green when one must stick to beige, or refusing to take down a satellite dish on the lawn or having three dogs when the bylaws say two per household is the limit.

"It's much easier to keep those communities up," says Debra Bass, vice president of the Community Associations Institute in Arlington, Virginia, which represents 150,000 homeowners' associations around the country. "And they increase in value at a faster rate than houses not in associations. People like the fact that there are rules about old cars in the driveway and how high the grass can be."

While homeowners' associations are increasingly common, and very popular, there are a few househunters—and some who have already moved into a community with these bylaws—who very definitely do not like what they see as an inability to express themselves or make personal choices. Those folks are in the minority, however. Most have no trouble adapting to covenants in the community they choose (after reading the bylaws carefully before buying, of course.)

You can start one of these associations if you have 100 percent of homeowners within your boundaries willing to form such a group. You would then hire a lawyer to do some research for you, and put together a nonprofit corporation. Or someone in your group might volunteer to do that work. He or she would contact your state's division of corporations, which will send a packet of material to read and forms to fill out. When you have completed the required process, anyone buying a home within your group's boundaries must join the association.

Ellen Hirsch, a Florida attorney in a firm that represents 2,600 homeowners' associations in that state, notes the growing popularity of "guarded" or "gated" communities as well.

These are made up of homeowners who for the sake of security choose to seal off all access to outsiders, usually by closing off through streets until there is just one entrance to the development. At the entrance might be a guard in a gatehouse, or gates that can be opened only by residents.

"Doing that has a serious impact on the whole community, not just those homeowners," Hirsch explains, noting that homeowners will have to hire a lawyer or choose one of the members to conduct traffic studies of the area they want closed off and hire an architect to design a guardhouse or otherwise redirect traffic flow, among other steps.

It is likely to be worth the time and money spent, however. Hirsch, who is also a member of the board of trustees of the Community Associations Institute, notes, "I've never heard of any municipality that did not eventually go along with this. It's really an easy way of soothing those citizens' concerns about crime. And it does significantly cut down on crime."

Hirsch adds not all homeowners in the area considered for closing off have to go along with the plan. If there are enough of those in favor to attract the attention of the local government representative, the closing off is likely to be okayed. Again, the ruling body is likely to see votes, votes, votes. Two hundred homeowners want it, seven do not? The closing off passes.

"There's no question that numbers of voters are necessary to get anything done," Hirsch concludes.

Simpler, Please

You don't want quite *that* formal an association, changes *that* drastic?

Then you might form a block or civic association, where membership is not mandatory, although you would of course like everyone to join. You do not have to have anything as major as closing off streets in mind. Perhaps you just want to make small changes in the community, charge $5 or $10 a year per household as dues for printing a newsletter or a flyer announcing a social event, and that's all.

Certainly you can do that successfully.

First, call a meeting open to anyone in the area you want to unite. If there is a reason for pulling together at this particular moment, that is even better. Perhaps you have been frustrated by city snow removal over the past winter and you want to make sure that sluggish performance is not repeated. So you form the First Ward Civic Association, approach your city council representative with your complaint, and request that the city snap to it in the upcoming winter months.

There might have been a number of burglaries in your area, and worried residents want to join together to see how they can fight crime. You could invite a representative from the local police department to address members at your initial meeting about crime-stopping measures they can take in and around their homes. Or there could be a low-cost home improvement loan program coming up you might want to know more about. You could invite someone from the city agency disbursing the monies to speak to your association. Or perhaps you have an absentee landlord whose property has become the local eyesore, and you want to band together to see what can be done. Any small or large neighborhood concern provides a good reason for uniting.

If everything is just fine where you are, you might want to join together to hold a block party in the summer. Or perhaps a huge neighborhood garage or lawn sale.

Some Notes and Suggestions

Once you are an association, there is no limit to what you can accomplish, both in improving the look of houses and streets within your borders and in getting together and enjoying yourselves at a variety of social events.

Here's just one example:

Pine Run is a 100-unit patio home community in the South. (With patio homes, residents own their own units plus their front lawns and backyards. In a condominium development, all grounds are common property.) Pine Run is nearing its tenth birthday now. Interestingly, its developer never set up a homeowners' association when it opened. Noting that void, some owners banded together seven years ago to form the Pine Run Betterment Association. Almost 80 percent of homeowners now belong to the association, but since that is not 100 percent, membership is not mandatory for those moving in. So while those in the association strongly urge members to obey the bylaws drawn up for the group, they are not legally enforceable (unless they coincide with existing city laws—leash laws for dogs, for example).

Still, the association has had a number of successes, is running smoothly and has made most homeowners maintain and noticeably improve their properties.

Helene Wilhelm, a block representative for the association, describes some activities and improvements the group has sponsored:

- Signs at the entrance to the community noting a crime watch program, and other signs stating a 30 MPH speed limit within its borders. "We asked for 20," Wilhelm recalls, "but we got 30." The group also got a "Dead End" sign in Pine Run's one cul-de-sac.
- A talk to members by a private corporation selling crime watch kits and speaking about personal safety in, around and away from the home.
- A talk to older members about health insurance.
- A "great-looking lawn"contest, including shrubbery and flowers—an award made monthly throughout the summer. Since summer runs seven months or longer in that part of the country, the contest stretches across a good chunk of the year. An attractive sign, made by a member, is stuck in the winning greenery and stays there for 30 days. That program, begun in 1994, "helped get a lot of people to spruce up their front lawns," Wilhelm said.
- An annual free dinner for members at a church across the street from the community, paid for from the annual dues of $30, which are also used for maintenance of the entryway of the development and printing the newsletter.
- A holiday home-decorating contest each December, with a winner announced for the most attractive exterior decorating.
- A monthly newsletter.
- Requests community residents have made in the bylaws, such as leash laws for pets, specific paint colors for all units, etc. Owners have willingly obeyed these requests. Some victories have come about simply by requesting homeowners' adherence to the covenants, others because the bylaws were similar to citywide prohibitions.

Some Ideas To Get You Rolling

- Every homeowner within the borders of the neighborhood you are binding together must be invited to join the association. Absentee landlords should be asked. Invite tenants too. Some will decline, but others will be quite concerned about the appearance of their neighborhood and will welcome the opportunity for input. You must be seen as a total representation of the neighborhood in question, not a clique.

- Ask small businesses to join, too, if there are some within your boundaries. They are likely to be just as concerned about the community as homeowners are.
- Keep it simple. You will need a president, a secretary to record minutes of meetings and a treasurer to handle dues. There can be a subchair for programs and events as they come up.
- Always, always, always listen to any member who wants to speak. Naturally, you will have to cut short what seems to be turning into a filibuster, but otherwise, let 'em talk.
- Dues should be as low as you can make them—$10 or $20 a year is common, if there is no money needed to hire a lawyer or conduct some other complicated business—and residents should know what that money is going to provide. Annual upkeep of some common area, perhaps? A newsletter? A summer block party? An emergency fund for a problem you see looming?
- Don't meet too often, unless you have a neighborhood crisis you are all seeing through. People do not like to attend meetings in these days that are so busy for us all. Some are particularly averse to—make that downright afraid of—going out to meetings at night.
- Is there a small plot of land within your association borders you could lobby local government to turn over to you for a community garden? Your county extension service can then help you with vegetables you might grow (see Chapter 5 for more about this office).
- Keep in touch with your elected officials. If you produce a monthly, bimonthly or quarterly newsletter, all your representatives should be on the mailing list.
- If your blocks need a face-lift, someone in the group might look into government programs or a local private contributor to help you spruce up the place.
- Neighborhood Watch is a popular program across the country, and might be a good one for your group to adopt. A close-knit low-crime neighborhood can make you feel better and have a positive effect on property values as well. If your local law enforcement agency cannot help you start one, two offices can. The National Crime Prevention Council (Department F-1, 1700 K St. NW, 2nd Floor, Washington, DC 20006) offers a free crime prevention packet, including booklets with crime preven-

tion tips. The National Sheriffs' Association (1450 Duke St., Alexandria, VA 22314) will send you a Neighborhood Watch Sample Kit, including decals and brochures on crime prevention, for $3, which covers postage and printing.

• You can send for the free CAI Resource Catalog from the Community Associations Institute (1630 Duke St., Alexandria, VA 22314). The catalog lists all CAI publications that can help you organize and run your association. Some titles: *The Homeowners' Association Manual, The You Can Do It! Newsletter Kit, Lighting Up for Safety and Security* and *Pet Peeves (and What to Do About Them),* for keeping the furry residents of your community well behaved.

SUMMING UP

$ It is preferable, but not absolutely necessary, to have a point of common concern to rally homeowners in forming an association.

$ Everyone in the area covered should be invited to join, including absentee landlords, tenants and business owners.

$ Keep in touch with local elected officials.

$ Enjoy yourselves! Have a variety of social events to keep you all in touch and united.

CHAPTER 3

The Roomer's
Going Around

Do you have a bedroom you're not using?

Consider taking in a roomer.

We are not talking about the Mrs. Murphy-style boardinghouse here, with strangers seated around the dinner table. For one thing, roomers do not take meals in the house—boarders do.

Also, the l990s style of roomer is the man or woman who comes to stay only for a while, so there are many times when you and your family have the house to yourselves.

What's Involved Here

When thinking about a roomer, you will want to talk with your accountant about the tax benefits (deductions for maintenance, repairs and depreciation for the part of the house you are renting on a long-term basis).

There are several avenues you can pursue to find the roomer you want, for the period of time you want him or her to stay with you.

Rosemarie Nervelle and her husband, Tom Laurent, have a young woman staying with them periodically in their New Jersey home that has become too large for them since the children have grown and gone.

The woman—we'll call her Sue—is in her 20s, and is employed by the Chicago office of a company based in one of the many office parks in the northern part of the Garden State. When she comes to New Jersey to visit that office, about once a week, she stays overnight in a room in Nervelle and Laurent's home.

"She's been with us now for four and a half years, and she's a wonderful young woman," says Nervelle. Sue's room, and her own bath, are on the first floor of the couple's home, while the other three bedrooms are upstairs. "I've given her kitchen privileges," Nervelle points out, "but she never uses them." Sue has her own house key, and comes "home" anywhere between 9:30 and 11 PM, after dinner conferences. The next morning she's gone—either to the New Jersey office or back to Chicago. That's it until the following week.

Nervelle came by her sometime roomer through a friend who works in the relocation department of Sue's company. Nervelle and her husband have a contract with the company for, Nervelle says, "over $100 a week" to put Sue up for as many as five times per week, although she is rarely there for more than a weekly overnight stay.

Nervelle talked to a company spokesperson before agreeing to take Sue, and suggests anyone else considering a corporate roomer do the same. "You can't be too careful," she points out. "If someone approaches you for a room, I'd say contact the company and ask them about the character of the person, how long they've been with the company, and then certainly interview that individual in person. I had the company CEO come with my roomer on her interview."

If you live in an area rife with corporate offices, this might work out well for you. Safety is a concern of business travelers today, especially women. That and an interest in being more comfortable in the endless round of corporate travel are two reasons bed-and-breakfast accommodations have begun seeing more business travelers over the last few years. Putting up long-distance commuters in private homes takes that lodging style a step further.

Sue, Nervelle says, is pleased to be staying in the couple's home rather than a motel. Her office is just a five-minute drive from where she rooms. And her husband told Nervelle he feels more comfortable knowing his wife is staying with the couple.

Nervelle says the question of Sue having guests over never arose. Her fiancé, whom she soon married, was in Chicago. You will have to determine how much entertaining you will allow your roomer.

Besides that issue, as a homeowner you will also have to address smoking versus no smoking in the guest's room, whether you will allow full kitchen privileges (for dinner, for example), or just morning access to that area. Nervelle supplies linen and housekeeping for the room, and you will be expected to do the same.

Since Sue is only an occasional guest in their home, the couple have no problem with neighborhood zoning. They are certainly not running a rooming house.

Getting Started

Try this if your home is near corporate offices with headquarters or branches in other cities. Those offices are apt to see a lot of inter-office travel among staff. It is unlikely a company will sign you up if you are more than 5 to 15 minutes away from their office, however. Your selling point will be your proximity to the office (plus, of course, your homey atmosphere and safety).

You can contact the personnel or human resources departments of the companies you are considering, and they should be able to direct you to the department or individual concerned with finding accommodations for traveling employees or others visiting their offices who must stay in town overnight. You may have to do a bit of a sales job, since some may not be familiar with the idea of placing employees in private homes.

Once you have convinced the corporate powers-that-be, and have interviewed a prospective roomer and a company representative, ask for a contract from the company. The contract should spell out the agreement and the company's responsibility for payment. If the contract allows for another employee to follow your current roomer when the time comes, be sure to specify you want to interview that employee before he or she arrives at your home to stay. You will not want that room open to anyone the company sends, any time it wishes.

The College Scene

Living in a college town offers a prime opportunity for finding a roomer who will stay with you longer than a corporate type is likely to, but will still be gone for holidays and in the summer if you specify that is what you want.

Claudia Logue took in two sisters, one attending college in her small northeastern city, the other working elsewhere in town full time. This was before she converted her three-story home to two full apartments (see Chapter 7). The lower level of the house had two bedrooms, one and a half baths, a storage room, sole access to the small backyard and no kitchen. The two young women had a separate entrance, too. The situation worked well for all.

"I would have liked them to stay longer because the rent money was good and they were good tenants," Logue recalls, "but at the end of the school year they took an apartment in town."

In setting a rent for her roomers, Logue had to keep in mind that, despite all the pluses the space had to offer, one roomer would have to pass through the other's bedroom to get to the bath with the shower. This was the major downside to Logue's finding two roomers for the floor, but fortunately the two sisters found it no drawback.

Logue set the rent at $380 per month, taking into account that small full one-bedroom apartments were renting in her community for around $500 to $600, some of them were walkups and most had no yard. If she had charged $60 per week per roomer—a typical room rent in her area at the time—she could have pulled in $480 per month. But because the two women were sisters and had no problem with the layout of the bedrooms and full bath, and because Logue knew it would be difficult to find two strangers who would accept that layout, she lopped off $100.

This landlord found it more convenient to charge by the month, but many homeowners charge their roomers by the week. Some roomers pay a one-week security deposit, others a one-month fee. Logue asked for and received a month's security.

There were no kitchen privileges attached to the rooms Logue rented, which is common with roomer situations. This worked out well for her tenants, too, since the young woman attending college took her meals at school, and her sister ate elsewhere in town.

Most of the time.

Logue says she saw a hot plate in their rooms, "and I saw some pizza deliveries, so I know they were eating in occasionally, but that didn't bother me."

Zoning was not a problem for Logue because her home was in a part of town with many large houses converted to two-, three- or even four-apartment units. Logue offered the girls a standard apartment lease, the kind available in any stationery store, amending it here and there (no pets, the term to run from late August to early June, etc.).

Logue's only concern with her tenants, she says now, was the jamming of electrical outlets she saw when she went downstairs.

"The house inspector who looked at the place when I bought it told me the electrical system was all right for a house built around 1920, but I still worried when I saw hair dryers, curlers, computers, radios, televisions, extension cords—every outlet, it seemed, full," she explains. "I did worry about overload, or their leaving something still turned on while they were out, but nothing dreadful happened."

You can find college students by advertising on bulletin boards at schools, or by calling the schools' residence halls or dorm offices, which usually keep lists of apartments available, and sometimes rooms for rent too. Housing on campus can be pretty hard to come by in some college communities, and occasionally those offices send out a call for homeowners to make some accommodations available. Those offices do not visit the apartments, however, or pass on them in any way. They just hand the student the name, address and rent asked, or sometimes they post homeowners' notices on bulletin boards within the dorm offices.

Naturally, you will interview anyone you are considering renting a room to, spell out the specifics of your rental situation, and make sure the student can afford the quarters you have to offer. How can you be sure that seemingly nice, polite 19-year-old can swing your rent each month? By having the parent's name on the lease, or having the parent cosign for the student, whichever makes more sense given the age of the student. The parent is likely to be paying the student's college expenses, including housing, anyway. Most are prepared to be as responsible for housing charges off-campus or on campus.

The Older Homeowner

There has been a growing movement over the last half-dozen years or so to help retirees remain in their homes by finding a roomer or housemate for them. State and local agencies have set up programs to match elderly homeowners with younger people who are looking for inexpensive housing, or with folks their own age who need to cut housing costs. You might find a roomer through these agencies. Perhaps, if you choose, it can be a young roomer who will do some household chores and/or lawn work for a lower monthly rent.

Contact your state office on aging in your state capital if you do not know of any local programs or agencies. Staffers there can put you in touch with offices near you that might not be familiar to you. The agencies make the match (of roommate or housemate or roomer) at no fee to the homeowner. They also draw up contractual agreements.

More Options

As you read this, many Atlanta homeowners are preparing to take in paying guests during the 1996 Summer Olympics. If a major sports event or other competition comes to your community, or perhaps a World's Fair or similar spectacular, you have an excellent opportunity for making money renting a room or two before that activity disappears.

Here's another idea, one implemented frequently around the country: if you live in a town with a regional or community theater, you can offer a room to the folks employed by the theater on a periodic basis.

Michael Stotts, managing director of the New Jersey Shakespeare Festival, based in Madison, New Jersey, is almost always on the look for homeowners to host his actors and technicians. But there is more involved here than an exchange of names and addresses. Stotts talks to would-be hosts on the phone, "and if it seems like it's going to work, we'll look at the house, to see who it would be suitable for in the company."

Stotts tries to get homes as short a distance as possible from the theater—the roomers will ride bicycles back and forth—but has been known to go as far as 20 miles away for housing.

Rents are negotiable, but because the theater is a nonprofit organization, Stotts naturally keeps his eye on the bottom line (the theater organization pays for the lodging of the actors and technicians). Ask too much for your quarters and you are likely to go to the end of the line, if you are called at all.

Some rentals, he says, are short—one week, say—while others are for the entire season, which runs 16 weeks.

Stotts suggests homeowners interested in renting rooms to theater staff, both onstage and behind the scenes, should contact the administrative offices of theater companies in their area.

The Shakespeare Festival theater is in a suburban, upscale area of New Jersey, one not exactly rife with roominghouses or other boarding possibilities. Which could be why Stotts says, "I wish there were more people out there to do this."

Do you live in a resort area? One where many young people are employed during the high season as waiters and waitresses, chambermaids, workers on the boardwalk or at the ski resort? Here, too, you can take in the occasional roomer, who will stay at your place just for the season. Contact hotels and resorts in your area who can pass along your vacancy to new employees.

What should you charge these folks? Check the classified section of your local paper under "Rooms to Let" for some idea of rates. Keep in mind the neighborhood or part of town advertising the vacancy, and also the season. The room close to the ocean that rents for $40 a week in a December ad will take an astronomical leap in July.

Finally, if you live within a few blocks of a large hospital or medical center, you might want to contact that facility's administrative office with the thought of putting up relatives of patients, or corporate visitors. A home-like atmosphere and being close to the facility are your selling points.

SUMMING UP

💲 Taking in a roomer does not have to be a year-round investment on your part. There can be a number of people who will want to stay at your place only occasionally.

💲 Consider every possible source for roomers—corporate offices, colleges, theater groups, resort hotels.

💲 Always interview your prospective roomer in person. Do not let companies, colleges, and the like send someone to fill your vacancy, with the understanding that you have no requirements other than filling that room.

CHAPTER 4

Your Office/
Your Home

I t's morning. Time to get to work. You grab your mug of coffee in the kitchen and make your way to the office—30 feet away, in another part of the house.

Whew, that commute'll kill you.

Wouldn't *you* like to join the nation's 24 to 39 million (estimates vary) workers who are based in their homes?

Earning a living from home *can* save money—rent on a place elsewhere in town, for instance.

Paul Darling is a photographer who has worked for several years from his Rhode Island home, or rather a small studio on the property. "I simply will not go downtown," he says. "It would cost me $500 to $800 a month to rent space." Darling adds that he needs no walk-in business with the work he does, so where he sets up shop is immaterial.

There are more savings with a home office: commuting costs and the money that seems so easily frittered away on lunches, clothes, office gifts, etc. The home office can also save a little on the expense of day care.

Finally, with the low overhead of a home office, you might be able to charge clients a little less than your competition.

It is impossible to discuss all aspects of a home office, down to the fine print on tax regulations, in one chapter. But you can certainly get an overview of this growing development on the national landscape, one you might want eventually to adopt as your own work style.

What's Involved Here

Naturally, there are jobs we can quickly eliminate from any consideration of home work. If you are selling men's clothing in a department store, you might as well turn to the next chapter (unless you have had in mind for some time starting a business that could be run from your house).

This section also does not address itself to employees who bring work home from the office only occasionally—paperwork they can do easily at the kitchen table or a desk in the bedroom.

The chapter is for those who are considering starting a home-based business, who are self-employed and want to move their operation home, who want to operate a sideline business from home, or who are salaried employees but "telecommute."

Give careful thought to creating an office in your home. Just because you *can* operate from your own quarters doesn't mean you *should*. The dentist with a thriving downtown practice might make life easier for himself by building a small wing onto his home that will become an office. If that means losing a whopping number of his patients, though, it is obviously a bad move. The dentist must feel such a drop is workable while building up a new suburban patient base. You will read so often throughout this book about the importance of location as it relates to your home and its value. Obviously it is vital to your business too.

The Community Steps In

You will want to investigate what is allowed where you are, but in general zoning officials tend not to mind home offices in residential neighborhoods where there will be no clients coming and going and taking up other residents' parking spaces. Occupations such as artist, writer and teacher have long been considered home businesses that cause no ripple in the neighborhood.

You might find your biggest adversaries will be your neighbors. No one who lives in a strictly residential community—probably not you either if this did not apply to you personally—wants to see a few businesses cropping up very obviously in residents' homes, lowering property values and changing the quiet appeal of the neighborhood.

If you live in a community with a homeowners' association, you will probably find your neighbors even less thrilled at the idea of your home business. Your bylaws might expressly forbid it. If belonging to an association is mandatory for moving into your community, whether it is single-family houses or condominiums, those bylaws are legally enforceable.

However, much depends on *how* you make your living. If you are a psychologist who will see patients one after the other, with no traffic congestion and indeed no one even knowing about or seeing any sign of your business, you are not stirring things up.

But if you start a highly visible business—for example, repairing cars in your driveway—your association can order you to shut down. This is especially likely if one or two neighbors complain—and one or two always will.

Do you live in a neighborhood that seems pretty mixed—homes, a few shops, storefront offices? Then local officials and the folks on your street are less likely to make it hard for you to set up a home office.

With certain types of home work you also will have to secure a business license from city hall or other local authorities.

If you need a name for your business, you will have to file that with the appropriate agency.

Starting Up

Here are a few points to consider about the personal side of a home business.

- Think about *why* you want to work from home. Saving on rent elsewhere? No more commuting? Cheaper because of all the little extras associated with going to work in the city or at the office park? Tired of the rat race? Car on its last legs? Remember, you have to truly believe you can make a success of this, and are not "settling" for home work. Which bring us to . . .
- This reason for working at home might be considered part of the above, but it deserves separate mention because it is increasingly common: working from home because of a new

baby, or a small child or two. There are many women these days—it is usually women—who decide to set up a home office so they can be there for the children, and can save on day care expenses. That can work for school-age kids. The family can well save on after-school babysitting or day care because someone is home between 2:30 and 6 PM.

Will it work if you have an infant or toddler?

It has for Jerri Hood of Moore, Oklahoma, who began her home-based word processing business to be near her children, who are now ten, five and two. She gave birth to both her second child and the business five years ago.

"It's easy to keep an eye on them," Hood says. "They're good kids."

Hood explained that from the glassed-in porch that is her office, she can watch the kids playing in the living room while she works. The house has been essentially childproofed, and other rooms are closed off during her work hours. "I get up often and look around," she says.

Hood breaks to have lunch with the kids, and then makes up for lost time by working a few hours in the evening.

There *have* been moments. If there is a child crying in the background when the phone rings, "I let the machine pick it up," she says. "I don't want to answer the phone with kids screaming."

Hood concedes, "I have to have so much stress in my life or I can't function. I thrive on it."

Would you? An assistant Hood has in periodically says *she* could not work like that with her child.

Keep this in mind if you are expecting a baby—and expecting a full-time home-based career while minding him or her.

Many women get around this problem by starting a home-based day care center of their own (there is more about this in Chapter 8). Stay home, take care of your own kids, and earn money tending one or two more!

• Are you a self-starter? There will be no one at home to motivate you. Especially if you are undertaking a new business, you must have all the skills that make for success in the marketplace, even though your marketplace is your converted den. If you are salaried, but work from home for your employer, you still need the spur to work that must come from inside yourself. Your superiors will expect you to keep up the same pace and produce the same results you would if you were in an office environment.

- You will have to make the family understand that you are not to be disturbed during working hours unless there is an emergency. And you will tell them ahead of time what you consider an emergency.

Your Office

It does not have to be fancy or expensive, just, well, workable.

You *will* need serious space that will not have to be dismantled when company comes for dinner. If you have no spare room or unused bedroom, you might consider creating a small nook in a room serving another purpose, perhaps separated from the rest of the area with a paneled screen or a folding door.

Anne Johnson is a freelance writer and boating columnist who lives with her husband on a 40-foot sailboat. She used to work in the newsroom of a daily paper, but now puts in long hours at her full-time home-based career, with all the requisite hi-tech gear. She feels not the least bit crowded.

"If you look at cubicles in a corporation," she points out, "they are about three feet by five feet. My office on the boat is four feet by six feet. How much more room do you need? All you really have to have is a little spot in a corner somewhere."

Furnishing Your Office

Wow! Wouldn't you like to be Fay Darling (who is married to Paul, the photographer we met at the beginning of this chapter), who won a completely furnished home office in a magazine-sponsored contest. Deliveries were made over several days of a desk, two side chairs, one "executive" chair, a computer, two lateral files, two bookcases, a telephone and even venetian blinds. She already had a fax machine, or that would have arrived at her door too.

Darling's office is an unused bedroom in the couple's house. Formerly an office manager, she now does bookkeeping for small companies in her area, and has begun branching out to desktop advertising and marketing for small businesses.

"One of the first things I would tell anyone working at home," Darling says, "is scope out all the decorating contests." They do not have to be offered by home office publications either. Darling won her booty from *Weekend Decorator* magazine.

Even without winning a contest, you can still have a well-furnished workplace on a budget.

Look around at used furniture stores and privately owned office supply stores (you won't find these at the superstore warehouses) for secondhand desks, chairs and file cabinets. There are some great buys to be had there and, occasionally, some wonderful old oak desks and file cabinets, if you like that look for your workplace.

However, keep in mind that a $10 chair is no bargain if it seems likely to give you a backache after a few hours.

And your computer had better fit into any workstation you buy secondhand, too.

If you are salaried and will be working at home, is your company paying for the computer equipment you will need? If not, Anne Johnson suggests you consider a secondhand machine. Johnson, who has state-of-the-art equipment herself (her husband works with computers), believes the only reason a home office worker would need a brand-new computer would be if he or she is in a cutting-edge business—a graphic artist, for example, or someone who designs and writes newsletters for a variety of clients.

"The average small-business person," Johnson says, "can use these secondhand machines for the next six or seven years. They don't wear out or run out. It's just that a lot of buyers want all the bells and whistles. Some people need that; most don't." Used computers can start as low as $200.

A fax machine might be a must with your work, but if it is not, and money is tight, you can always use a nearby service. Depending on the type of business you have, you might want to have a two-line telephone. You definitely will need an answering machine. A two-line machine costs around $100.

Make this environment, where you will be toiling away so many hours, as attractive as you can. Add framed prints, plants or anything else it takes for you to enjoy walking into that space each day.

The Downside

Even those who love working at home concede there are some negatives to the work style:

- The major downside if you are planning to start your own business is, of course, the lack of a regular paycheck. Obviously, you will have considered that and will have some cushion or a second income in the household to see you through the early start-up days.
- "I'm a little isolated," says Paul Darling. "It's really up to me to make my contacts. But I'm only a telephone call away from the people in my business."

  "One of the things I miss are the social contacts I had on a daily basis," Fay Darling notes. "You don't have any reason really to go out of the house if you have your work there."

  Interesting, isn't it, how both Darlings feel the isolation of home work, even though they do in some respects work together at home. What is missing for both here is the lack of workplace chatter and gossip, folks in your business off whom you bounce ideas. The Darlings are in different professions, which lends an isolation of its own to their workdays, even though they may be under the same roof at times.

  For many home workers that aloneness is no problem, is even welcome. If you are very much a social animal, however, you may find this work style so totally impossible you will run screaming back to the noise and bustle of your downtown office.
- If you are not salaried, you will have to pay your own health insurance, which can be a monumental outlay of cash each year. One solution: join as many professional associations as you can, to qualify for inclusion in a group plan with one of them. The Darlings, for example, have been able to secure coverage they consider satisfactory through membership in their local chamber of commerce.
- You may find yourself *too* much into your business, not so much in the hours you put in, but in the attitude you send business contacts and prospects that says "Call me any time you want, any time at all."

  That is not particularly professional, not to mention draining to you. Let your answering machine take calls after normal business hours, even though you might be right there at your desk plugging away. If you receive business calls over the weekend, tell the caller you will phone back first thing Monday morning. They will respect you for setting limits.

Women working at home are often taken advantage of because they are there all day. Here, too, while you will have to do your fair share of carpooling and community activities, you will also have to learn to say no if you feel neighbors are infringing on your time and good nature.

- Finally, an important downside, especially for those who are salaried and working full-time, or even a few days a week, from home: You are out of the loop, and that can mean a slowdown in career progress. That does not apply to everyone in every career, but if you think it could be a consideration in your work situation, then do stop and give it some thought.

Insurance

Do not neglect this important aspect of running a home-based business. Yes, you can increase coverage on the property portion of your homeowners policy, perhaps with a special rider for all the equipment you have bought. But you probably need special coverage for your particular work situation, too.

Paul Darling recalls an incident when he was shooting wedding pictures away from home, and "a little grandmother collided with me. She was frail, and fell down immediately. Her son was a lawyer. Fortunately my insurance carried through to my working on location."

Talk to your agent about exactly what your business is at home and away from home. You do not want to topple an elderly grandmother whose son is a lawyer, without adequate protection.

The Tax Situation

Yes, there are tax benefits to having a home office, but perhaps maybe not as many as you would think, and the area is a continually changing one. Your business must first of all have a profit motive to qualify for home office deductions. Your home office must be your primary business location; it must be used to meet clients if that is what your business involves and it must be an exclusive area of your home (not the kitchen table).

If you are just starting out, your accountant can, of course, help you set up shop tax-wise. Anyone working at home can call the IRS at 800-829-1040 to ask specific questions and request copies of the many booklets they offer home workers.

One note before moving on to the next point, a caution that can definitely save money. If you are selling your home soon, consider not deducting your home business expenses the year of the sale. You will be hit with a tax penalty for the business part of the house. If you plan to use the "55 or over" $125,000 tax exemption, it would be better not to deduct *two* years' home business expenses before the sale.

Your New "Colleagues"

Well, now that you are working at home, you can no longer hang around with those wild and crazy guys at the water cooler. No matter. You now have a raft of new people and offices to help keep you in the mainstream, updated on developments in your field, and in touch with those who are in circumstances similar to yours.

- Join as many trade and professional associations as you can. Not just the national ones, although they can offer important assistance. Join groups in town. They have benefits galore, too, both monetary and social.

  They can stir up new business for you, for one thing, and help you see your business or service as part of the larger picture in your community.

  "They're your network," says Johnson, the freelance writer who lives on a sailboat. "You need somebody to give you that 'atta boy' support, and get you out of the house."
- Subscribe to publications that can help you, such as magazines and newsletters directed at your work specialty. Both Johnson and Fay Darling mentioned how invaluable the monthly magazine *Home Office Computing* has been to them. You do not have to have a computer to get a lot from this publication. It covers marketing, payment problems, insurance, loans and every other subject of interest to the home worker. "When it comes in the mail I drop everything and read it," says Johnson.
- Keep in regular communication with your regional office of the U.S. Small Business Administration (SBA). The SBA offers printed material for the small-business owner and loans that can help you get off the ground. If you are a minority or a woman starting a business, the SBA can be especially helpful. The office also offers seminars and training. For more information, call 800-8-ASKSBA.

SUMMING UP

$ A home-based office may save you the rent of an office down-town, and auxiliary expenses as well.

$ Zoning officials will be interested in your home office, but your neighbors are likely to be more concerned.

$ Know yourself and your home situation—your temperament, support from the family, etc.—well enough to be sure this is workable.

$ Reach out to local professional and trade associations to become your new support system—and a possible source of new business.

CHAPTER 5

Xeriscaping and Other Lawn Money-Savers

Have you noticed how much it costs to maintain a front lawn, keeping it attractive enough so it does not become the topic of neighborhood tsk-tsking? And then there is the backyard, which, while not on display, still needs a minimum effort on your part to keep it from becoming an overrun jungle or a dreary sandlot.

There is fertilizer to buy, and grass plugs, plant food, bug sprays (different kinds for different critters), weed killer, plus a mower, edger, blower, new plants, plants to replace the new plants that died, sod, flowers, mulch, hoes, rakes, fertilizer spreader . . . if they sell it, well, you really should buy it . . . shouldn't you? What kind of neighbor are you, anyway?

Funny thing, though. All those products taking up so much space in your garage or basement, and your lawn is still not exactly contest material. What can be done to put you back in charge, short of filling in the whole space with Astroturf or paving it over for a few more parking spaces?

(An aside here. Those who enjoy puttering around the lawn and yard—and it can be a relaxing hobby, not to mention good exercise—will find several money-saving tips in this chapter that will not curb their pleasure, only their spending.)

What's Involved Here

You *can* call a halt to the madness that keeps you a slave to your lawn, constantly forking out money. While initially it will take a little work and some cash, your efforts *will* pay off.

You have probably seen the word "xeriscaping" several times over the last few years. What does it mean? Well, the word is derived from the Greek *xeri*, meaning dry. Today, xeriscaping is a style of landscaping that calls for minimal watering, mainly by keeping plants and trees calling for the same watering schedule together.

Little watering means a lower water bill for you, of course, and also less attention you have to pay to your lawn. Not bad. But ee-eeeuw, you say, does that mean I have to have a yard full of cactus and sand?

You can if you want to. But the typical xeriscaped lawn can be as green and lush and colorful as you want. Think, to take one example, of the English country garden. Or a yard with a pond, if you choose, with water lilies. Judiciously placed mulch, rocks, pebbles, brick and cobblestones also can become permanent landscaping, eliminating the need to buy—and replace—costly shrubbery.

The varieties of landscaping that can go into a low-maintenance lawn are limited only by your imagination—or that of your designer.

This is a lawn that will have to be planned carefully, however, taking a number of factors into account. You must place plants needing the same amount of water together and consider climate zone, exposure to the sun, etc.

It should be noted here that one can take xeriscaping too far. Trying too hard to save water drives some homeowners to extremes in their yard planning, so it is important to keep this all in perspective.

Rob Layton, co-owner of Design Concepts, a Boulder, Colorado, landscape architectural firm, has done analyses on xeriscaping, and notes, "Savings depend on what water costs you where you are. In some places it's going to take you longer to amortize what you buy because some areas have higher water rates than others.

"Also, your air-conditioning bills are going to go up if you have white rocks all around your place," he continues. "You need the cooling effect of some plants and trees. But in areas you rarely walk into, like side yards, there's no point in maintaining a nice lawn. Go with rocks or mulch."

If you want to xeriscape all of your front lawn, or even a sizable chunk of it, you will need guidance, in the form of a comprehensive design. That will cost money if you call in a landscape designer or other professional, although the cost will balance out over the life of your new lawn. You can see that adding cobblestones or a brick wall to your lawn area, and lily ponds and waterfalls, might be beyond the skills of the average homeowner. Even the proper choice of low-maintenance plants and shrubs might call for professional assistance.

Your Low-Cost and No-Cost Helpers

You have several choices in looking for help from someone who knows more than you do about upgrading your lawn. Some of them are quite economical too.

- Most countries have a cooperative extension service. These offices offer expert advice on changes you want to make with your lawn. The folks working there know *everything* about grass, trees, bushes, flowers, and fruit and vegetables, too. And insects that plague the gardener. Their information is free, and they might offer printed material as well as answer your questions over the phone. This office is listed in your telephone book under County Government, or perhaps under Department of Agriculture.

    There is more about how this staff can help you in Chapter 15. You might be interested in their "master gardener" program, which is explained in those pages.
- Look to a landscape design student, who will certainly charge less than a full-fledged designer to work on your lawn. A good student is likely to be eager for the work—and the money. Visit colleges and universities in your area that offer a major in landscape design, and put up a notice on those schools' bulletin boards. You can call the head of the department, too. He or she may or may not want to make a specific recommendation, but you might still get answers to any questions you might have about an applicant you are considering, and the professor might also pass your notice around to a select few students.
- In one South Florida area, a local water management district office paid half the $4,000 cost of a xeriscaped lawn for homeowners who applied to that office to have their yards fitted with

water-saving plants and a new irrigation system. Naturally, if you want only a small portion of your lawn converted and do not want to go with an in-ground irrigation system, you will pay far less than that. If you have such an office near where you live, by all means give them a call to see what they offer home-owners who are interested in water-conserving lawns.

- You might want to take a course in landscaping your lawn, or even xeriscaping, if one is offered at your local community college or at an adult education program sponsored by your school board. For less than $100—and sometimes for as little as $10—you can not only learn from what the teacher has to say, but can also ask questions about your own plot of land.

  Laurie Prescott, who owns a landscaping firm in north Florida, teaches frequently at those schools, and says she *expects* to answer students' specific questions about their own yards and lawns. The most frequently asked question: "No doubt about it," Prescott says, "It's 'What will grow in the shade?'"

- Make friends with the best salesperson you can find at a good nursery. If you keep going back for purchases, and picking that individual's brain, it's like having your own landscape assistant. And it's free.

  "I spent $125 for camellia plants," recalls Janet Kovak of her attempts to fix up the lawn in front of her Georgia home when she moved there from the Northeast. "They died in three weeks. I couldn't believe it. It wasn't just temporary replanting shock, they were *dead*. I read the little tag that came with them, and it seemed to me they'd do all right, but when I got to talking to the guys at the garden center, I learned why camellias wouldn't have taken where I planted them. Now I spell out exactly, to someone there I have since found knows *everything*— where the plant will go, the exposure, the trees around it, whether the roof overhang will put it in the shade—anything that can affect its growth."

- Read. A lot. In the Gardening section of bookstores in your area you will find many books on the subject of water-saving lawns, xeriscaping, low-maintenance plants and shrubs—help for any situation or project you would want to undertake. If you have been an interested, and fairly clever, gardener for some time, the illustrations and text might guide you in designing your own lawn with no outside help. (If your skills do not extend to laying brick, you will have to call for a professional, of course.)

- Finally, drive around your own community. Or perhaps you will have to look no further than a house down the street. When you find a lawn you admire, whether for the greenery or the wood border or whatever, stop and chat with the homeowner/gardener. He or she is likely to be delighted at your admiration, and if the green-thumber personally made those installations, might offer you guidance in doing the same for yourself. And who knows, perhaps he or she would be willing to do your lawn, for a fee that is likely to be better than what a pro would charge.

Keep in mind as you are reading all this, and thinking about your own plot, that you do not have to make a huge conversion to a water-conserving or money-saving lawn all at once. Taking things slowly, in stages, can help you become used to your new lawn areas as they are completed, can give you time to make new choices and, perhaps most important, allow you to put together the money needed for the next stage. You should, however, be working from an overall plan, regardless of who designs it—the writer of a magazine article you've read, your county cooperative extension service, etc.—and not making changes willy-nilly. Mistakes cost money.

The Landscape Designer

If you are truly a stranger in a strange land when you wander out to your front lawn, and reading gardening magazines does nothing for you, and you can afford to go with the pros, by all means consider hiring a landscape designer. Yes, this is spending money, but there are savings to be realized here, too. For one thing, you will save in not having to keep buying new bushes, trees and plants for the ones that die!

The professional in this area might be called a landscape architect, like Rob Layton. These individuals are now licensed in 45 states. They usually work on big jobs, such as greenscaping around commercial buildings and residential developments, but they can also be retained by individual homeowners.

Landscape designers, on the other hand, are not regulated, although they have usually had some formal training in their field. They do both the design and contracting work themselves, sometimes with a work crew.

You can call in a designer if you can't seem to make anything stay alive, let alone grow; if you have no time to tend a lawn; or if you are looking for the perfectly xeriscaped lawn to realize the greatest time and money savings.

Homeowners who are about to move might also turn to a pro. A drop-dead lawn will pay you back come resale time. The Weyerhauser Company has conducted studies that show for every dollar spent on landscaping, homeowners can recover as much as $2 in increased home value. An attractive lawn is also likely to help a home sell more quickly.

A professional will "do" your lawn with anything else you want added besides grass. If you do not know exactly what you want, he or she can help you decide, given the soil, exposure, etc., of that green (or brown) space, very often using computer graphics.

How can you find the right designer for you? Getting recommendations from friends and neighbors is the time-honored method of finding any good tradespeople or craftspeople. You might stop by houses with good-looking lawns, too, and ask those owners if their lot was professionally designed and who did the work.

You can be charged an hourly fee or a flat rate here. The flat rate usually works out better for you. One charge you will be quoted is likely to be for the landscaper analyzing and making suggestions for what you might buy and where to place it. A second fee the landscaper will mention is if you require him or her (and a crew) to do the planting for you. If you think you can plant the bushes, plants and so on yourself, that will certainly be a money-saver. But don't be penny-wise and pound-foolish here. If you really don't think you can handle planting a $200 seven-foot tree, or anything else come to think of it, let the pro go ahead and do the entire job.

Tell the person you are considering your budget limitations, and ask for a "not to exceed" total price, so you know what this job is likely to cost you.

Will the landscaper guarantee the work and the plants? For how long? How much of the early maintenance will be your responsibility? Be sure you are given detailed maintenance instructions, and the designer you choose is amenable to coming back if problems arise, or is available for answering questions over the phone.

Some Other Money-Saving Tips

There are all sorts of opportunities for saving around your lawn and yard.

- Do you have a sprinkler system? Do you see it shooting out water immediately after a rainstorm? Or, even more bizarre, while it is raining? You can buy a moisture sensing gauge, which is a device you connect to the irrigation system. It automatically turns off the sprinkler when the gauge has enough water (like after a shower). That means your lawn has enough water too. When the gauge dries out, it turns the sprinkler back on. Cost: $10 to $15 at your home or garden center.
- Do you pay to have your grass cut? If you can do it yourself, that's a sizable saving each month.
- A compost pile—grass clippings, leaves and kitchen waste—will save you money on fertilizer and mulch. Your cooperative extension service can help with details.

Laurie Prescott, the Florida landscape designer, offers these tips:

- Ground cover, such as crape myrtle, certain ivies and the like, needs less fertilizer and water than grass does.
- Another idea for no-cost mulch: You might be able to get cypress mulch or pine bark from tree surgeons or municipal agencies that trim trees. They shred branches as they prune them or cut them down, and in many instances give the mulch away at no cost.
- Start small if you do not mind the wait. Buying smaller shrubs and flowers will be less costly than the larger or full-grown size, and will eventually grow to the look you want.
- Have friendly neighbors? Ask for cuttings of greenery you admire, and root them at your place. Cost: nothing.
- Grass seeds or plugs are less expensive than sod.
- The wildflower garden (also known as the English country garden), if it will take where you live, is an attractive look with lots of color but costs little. All you really need to do is scatter seeds. Not a lot of maintenance when it's grown, either.

Gardening Tools and Gizmos

If you have a small patch of a yard, and want to be among the truly trendy, buy a hand-powered lawn mower. They are making a comeback these days. Push-mowers are cheaper to buy (typically less than $100, versus $250 or more for many power mowers); they do not pollute the air the way power mowers do; they are cheaper to run and today's styles cut better than the circa 1955 ones. That allows you to leave the clippings on the lawn to decompose and return nutrients to the soil, which cuts down the need to buy chemical fertilizers.

Another idea that might be a possibility where you live involves saving on tools. Yes, you can afford a hoe and hedge clippers. You probably do need your own mower. And neighbors might not be too happy with your continually borrowing an edger and blower. But what about other purchases that go into creating and maintaining the lawn?

Rob Layton suggests a few of you band together and buy some equipment, like a drop spreader for fertilizing, which is used only three or four times a year. Someone with a tool shed or space in the garage can store it.

Another suggestion: Look into renting seldom-used tools and machinery. You can keep even rental costs down if a few of you arrange to use that item during its two- or three-day rental period.

Some Reading

The Professional Lawn Care Association of America, a national trade association of approximately 1,000 lawn care companies, offers a free booklet, "What You Should Know About Lawn Care Products and Services." Send a self-addressed, stamped envelope to PLCAS at 1000 Johnson Ferry Road NE, Suite C-135, Atlanta, GA 30068.

The "Consumer's Guide to Hiring a Landscape Architect" (California Department of Public Affairs) is available at no charge from the California Board of Landscape Architects, 400 R St., Suite 4020, Sacramento, CA 95814. Yes, it was written for Californians, but the tips are so general they can help homeowners anywhere around the country.

Finally . . .

For more tips on water conservation, for your lawn and all around your house, see Chapter 10.

SUMMING UP

$ To hold down water bills, and other lawn care expenses, try xeriscaping.

$ Have a master plan for your chunk of greenery before making serious changes in layout.

$ Shop around for low-cost help.

$ When going with a landscape designer, have questions prepared before interviewing those professionals.

$ Whatever outdoor work you are doing yourself, enjoy! Take time to smell the roses—and all your other flowers.

CHAPTER 6

Share and Share Alike: Taking In a Housemate

Is your house too large for your needs these days, not to mention too expensive?

Perhaps you are newly divorced or separated, you've "inherited" the house that was once yours together and you would like to stay—if you can swing the costs.

Or you might be retired and want to remain in the same house where you have lived for many years.

Or you are just starting out in a career, have bought a condominium and now find, whew, owning a home is *expensive.*

If you fit one of the above profiles, can you stay where you are and still be relieved of steadily climbing house bills?

You can indeed. By sharing some of your space, you can reap at least $200—perhaps much, much more—a month to help with maintenance costs. Yes, you will be giving up some space, but it isn't being used anyway, is it? And, probably more important to you, there will be a loss of privacy too. But if you want to stay just where you are now, read on. While many ways of making and saving money are noted in this book, taking in a housemate might guarantee you one of the highest *regular* monetary returns, without making any structural changes in your home the way creating a separate apartment would.

What's Involved Here

First, let's look at all the "good stuff" involved in sharing. There certainly are a great many more positive aspects to this living arrangement than there are downsides.

- You will have companionship. It is believed that a fair number of Americans are sharing their homes more for this reason than for help with expenses. They want *someone* at home. This can be especially true for the newly divorced who are not used to living alone, and for the elderly, who for health reasons are more comfortable knowing there is someone else in the house.
- Having a housemate who is paying rent each month can lead to other savings too—sharing a grocery bill, for example.
- There is the safety factor in having another person around, a point not to be sniffed at these days.
- You might be able to work out a no-charge babysitting arrangement with your housemate if you are both parents. Or if you have no children, you could pick up some extra change babysitting your housemate's child.
- If you take in a student as a housemate (one who has use of the house on equal footing with you, as opposed to a roomer, an opportunity considered in Chapter 3), you might agree to accept babysitting services and/or tutoring and/or minor home repairs in exchange for lower rent.

Sounds good, doesn't it?
Ah, but what about the flip side to all those perks?

- Sharing your home will, even in the largest of houses, mean opening it up to a stranger, with that attendant lack of privacy.
- Your new housemate might want to bring some of his or her furniture, mixing and matching with yours, which might not be entirely to your liking.
- There is always the possibility your new housemate might have trouble coming up with the rent money once in a while,

although a careful check of references, and heeding your own vibes when interviewing, should make that less likely.

Rules, Regs and Taxes

While this idea is still new in your mind, better check to see if you *can* take in a housemate before considering it any further as a money making option.

It is not against zoning laws for two unrelated people to live together. However, if you plan to seek more than one housemate, or if you will be looking for a different housemate each year (as when a different college student lives with you during each school year), your neighbors may be alarmed at what seems like a boardinghouse arrangement.

If you are in a single-family or condominium community bound by covenants, you will have to look them over too. If no one has paid attention to the bylaws where you live for ages, that does not mean someone will not sound an alarm the minute you take in a sharer.

You will also want to check with your accountant to see how sharing will affect your tax situation. If you are over retirement age, you will also want to contact your Social Security office or your regional or state office on aging to see how sharing will affect benefits you are now receiving.

Finding a Sharer

All's well with the aforementioned suggestions?

Then let's get to the hunt for a housemate.

If you are of or beyond retirement age, you can contact your local or state office on aging. As discussed in Chapter 3, many communities around the country now provide match programs for senior citizens who want to remain in their own homes. Sometimes they will make the introductions to potential sharers; in other instances they will merely provide a listing of names. Some offices match only seniors with seniors; others will help seniors find an adult sharer in any age group.

If you are younger than 65 or so, *you* can contact those offices and agencies, too, since many seniors request sharers younger than they.

Retirees and homeowners of any age also can look for a housemate at the obvious places—work, including volunteer activities; house of worship; day care center; senior center; Parents Without

Partners and the like. Asking might not be enough, though. Put a notice on the bulletin board. And see if you can run a small classified advertisement in that group's newsletter.

Finally, many towns have roommate placement agencies, which also match house sharers. If yours does, by all means call or visit. But remember, while agencies can supply data about applicants and can refer them to you, it is up to you to do the screening necessary to find a compatible sharer. Usually, but not always, the individual looking for a house to move into pays the agency fee, which is often a percentage of a month's rent.

Sharing this time around is not like living with a college roomie when you were in school, or with several of the girls or guys in your first big-city apartment. Things are different now, as you know only too well. *You* are different, have different needs and requirements for a sharer and certainly very different obligations this time around. For one thing, you have that mortgage you weren't encumbered by in your youth! And that's not even getting into your *sharer's* past life, present needs, family and financial situation.

Successful matches are common, of course, with many sharers forging friendships that last long after the need to split expenses has passed.

Jane Saks, a single parent of a two-year-old daughter, took a housemate into her Massachusetts home a year or so ago. Her sharer is another single mom.

"In a normal sharing situation," she recalls, "you're looking for somebody you're compatible with. But here, I had to like the parent, we had to agree on parenting styles, and I had to like the child. It adds about nine more dimensions to the process."

Another point she had to consider: "I had bought this house when I was married, so it was completely furnished. Most women had their own style of decorating, and would have had to like mine. Some had their own furniture too.

"I interviewed men, and in some ways that would have been easier, but in other ways more complicated. Most men I saw were divorced, and didn't have furnishings, so that would have been the easier part. But with male sharers you have to walk a fine line. You have to like each other well enough to live together, but . . ."

Saks adds she "went with the first person who felt right, which happened to be another mom.

"Clearly the most important part of the process is finding someone who is willing to sit down and negotiate," she concluded.

That is what you will be looking for too—flexibility, someone of reasoned judgment, a sense of responsibility and, let us hope, a sense of humor.

What should you charge for rent? Look through the classified advertisements of your local paper to see what apartments are commanding where you live, and then scale your rent to take into account your sharer will not have the privacy of his or her own space that even an efficiency apartment would afford. Other factors to enter into your fee: the size of your house; how much space and privacy you are offering (Saks, for example, has two bedrooms for herself and her daughter on one floor, two for her housemate and her child on another, with all four sharing one and a half baths); whether the renter can bring some of his or her own furniture; whether he or she will have garage space and so forth.

Your jottings should list all your offer's good points, and then the ones that go on the debit side of the ledger (if your housemate will have to share your bedroom, or sleep on the living room sofa bed, for example). Keep in mind, though, that *you* are carrying the mortgage and responsibility for the house, including payment of real estate taxes, utility bills and possibly sewage and other charges. Just dividing in half an $800 monthly mortgage bill may not be fair to you.

The Agreement

Once you both have agreed on items like rent, space to be occupied by the housemate, length of the contract or lease, utilities, pets, smoking and use of alcohol, entertaining and overnight guests, groceries, housekeeping (who does it and how much), lawn and yard maintenance and anything else, *no matter how small the matter seems now*, have your agreement looked at by an attorney or by the social services agency that has been coordinating the match for you. A document, whether you call it a contract or agreement or lease, is vital. You can add riders to it as other issues crop up.

Your agreement can run five or more single-spaced pages. One full page will describe the premises—who is to live where, description of major pieces of furniture and who owns what. The agreement will describe the grounds, too, and who has access to what. Sound like too much trouble? But how much easier to refer to the contract when there is a disagreement or question about who does what or who owns what.

If you want to skip the expense of a lawyer, and you are not involved with a social services agency, you can purchase a standard apartment lease from a stationery store, and either use it with a lengthy rider spelling out all the topics that pertain to your situation, or write a new agreement using some of the points in that lease to guide you in points to be covered. Keep in mind, though, that those standard leases are more commonly used by landlords for tenants who do not live with them.

Finally . . .

Do you really think this money-maker can work for you? Here is a short quiz to see just how likely you are to live happily (platonically) with someone else—and perhaps with that someone's children, too:

- Are you reasonably self-sufficient, or are you looking for a sharer who will take care of you? Better not be. Mutual self-sufficiency is the key to success here.
- Do you need a lot of time to yourself that simply closing the door to your own room will not satisfy?
- If you are at or beyond retirement age, will you require your sharer to do more than he or she will expect when moving in— that is, maintenance of the house and lawn, driving you to this place and that, cooking and the like? Tell interviewees your requirements up front. Don't spring surprise requests after your sharer has moved in.
- If sharing with children, are you willing to pay attention to all the kids in the house? Successful sharers say the system works only in stable households in which the children are made an important part of things.

  Also on the subject of kids, if you have one or two (or more), you will probably find that prospective sharers who do not have children are not likely to be interested in your place. Similarly, if you have no children, you probably won't be too thrilled to see a young parent set up a playpen and other kiddie paraphernalia in your living room—and almost everyplace else too.
- Are you the sort who will label your own eggs and your cartons of yogurt in the refrigerator? That might work with another adult, but if you have children in the household there will be a

casualness about who owns what that you might not be able to handle.

- Is your financial situation so grim you are considering taking in a sibling to share, even though the two of you never really got along? You are not likely to find things going more smoothly now that you are forced to share a household.

- Are you basically a generous person, or are you going to count how many times you replaced lightbulbs to how many times he or she did? Naturally, almost every aspect of your sharing arrangement should be spelled out in black and white, but if you are the type to nickel-and-dime others to death, better pass on this money-saving strategy.

- Will you be careful to make sure you and your sharer are in pretty much the same financial boat? Poor Pearl living with Lady Muchbucks guarantees tension.

- Are you away from home a great deal, on business, perhaps? Bring that to the attention of a prospective sharer. Some will like having the house to themselves frequently, others will not. All should know in advance.

- Do you and your prospective sharer have the same values? If you're a straight shooter and he's bragging about ripping off everyone from city hall to the IRS, incompatability looms.

- Are you Felix or Oscar? Know thyself so you can inform a prospective sharer. "The Odd Couple" was a riot on television. You might find living the roles not at all amusing.

- Finally, after you have taken this quiz, pass it on to the person you are considering taking into your home, so you can see where your differences lie and whether they are serious enough to derail you.

SUMMING UP

$ Be sure you are temperamentally suited to having a housemate before beginning the search.

$ Look into your town's zoning ordinances and check your home-owners' association covenants if you are in such a community to be sure you *can* take a sharer.

$ Check references of applicants, but go with your own vibes too.

$ Draw up a contract spelling out *everything* involved in this arrangement, from laundry to lawn mowing.

CHAPTER 7

Landlording
Without Grief

This could be one of the best money-makers of all.

Do you have a large house, with more than a room going unused or underused?

Yes? Then do consider having a fully equipped rental apartment under your roof (actually, you would then have two full apartments, since where *you* live would become a unit as well). That rent can, depending on where you live, range from $300 to—well, $1,200 or more each month is not unheard of in some urban areas and college towns.

The rent can pay a good chunk of your mortgage, perhaps some of your property taxes too. Think how you will feel knowing that check is coming in each month—a sizable chunk of money, and you didn't even have to moonlight for it! You will probably go many, many months, too, without having to do anything, or at least very much, in the way of maintenance or repairs to the new apartment (if you start with a well-functioning unit). And while your fixed mortgage payment remains the same, you will be able to make rent increases periodically, so your income will continue to rise to keep pace with continually growing expenses in other parts of your life.

Having an apartment to rent can be a particular relief for those in precarious professions—the self-employed, for example, and those whose positions are always in danger of cutback or subject to the whims of the marketplace. No matter what happens at your place of business, the rent check will be slipped under your door each month. There will be at least *that* money coming in to keep you afloat in the event of a layoff or other financial catastrophe.

Claudia Logue is a freelance graphic artist living in a small, older city in the Northeast. She bought a three-story house in need of work, considering it an investment and, when she finished converting it to a two-family unit, a tidy little income producer as well. The first year in the house, Logue rented the lower floor to two roomers (see Chapter 3). A year later, after she got her bearings, she converted the two lower floors into a duplex apartment, so the bigger money could start rolling in. She lived on the third floor, a two-bedroom unit.

"I don't have a high income,"Logue explains, "and I doubt I'll ever make a fortune. So it's wonderful to know that rent check will be there every month. I'm getting $1100 a month now, which pays my mortgage and some of my real estate taxes."

There is more good news about becoming a landlord. The repairs and new installations you make to that rental unit are tax deductible. The apartment's share of your repairs to the house as a whole—a new roof, for example—are also deductible. So, if you live on two floors of the house and the tenants on one, one-third of the price of that roof can be deducted. Check with your accountant for the latest on this, and on depreciation allowances.

Of course there is a flip side to all this. There *will* be people—strangers at that—stomping around above you or below you, in *your home*. If you have lived in an apartment building, or a house converted to two or more apartment units, you can face that intrusion with equanimity. Otherwise, you are likely to find it disquieting. But only at first. Soon it will become familiar, and so almost unnoticeable.

Another consideration: Private homes converted to two or three separate living units do not usually appreciate in market value as quickly as single-family houses do. They can also take somewhat longer to sell when you are ready to move. That should not bring you too much inconvenience, however, since real estate is not a liquid investment and selling the most desirable house, even in one day, will not bring you instant cash.

What's Involved Here

You will have to check to see that a conversion is possible, not only in your neighborhood, but in your *block*. Restrictions can vary that narrowly. If a conversion is not permitted, you will have to try for a zoning variance to allow you to turn a single-family house into a two-family one. Variances can be very hard to come by, if not impossible, in some strictly residential neighborhoods. Occasionally an exception will be made for homeowners who want to create what is known as a mother-daughter or in-law apartment, where a dwelling unit is created for the parent of one of the homeowners. When Mom or Dad is no longer living in that flat, the house must revert to single-family status.

There are plenty of neighborhoods, however, where 1) zoning is lax throughout town, causing you no problem with your conversion and 2) variances can be secured in specific neighborhoods. So if you like this idea, it's certainly worth a try.

You? A Landlord?

You might be able to divide your house, but can you become a landlord? You must be very responsible indeed and very business-like, too—to undertake this venture. For example, if something is broken in that apartment, you must fix it, and promptly. You can put pots on the floor to catch water from a leaky roof in *your* unit, but you had better fix the roof that rains on your tenants pronto. It is the ethical thing to do, and if you do not, the tenants will run to city hall to lodge complaints against you.

Claudia Logue recalls, "There have been so many times I've looked at wallpaper for my apartment, or a rug for one of the rooms, but I usually have to let it go because the tenants need something. Not something nice, something essential, like a plumbing repair. I can only relax and buy for myself when things are caught up in their apartment."

You also need the disposition—no, sometimes the *stomach*—for landlording. Confronting a tenant behind in the rent. Complaining about too much noise from the rental unit. Handling a tenant's mistreatment of some part of the apartment. You need to be tough, tough, tough in this business.

Will You Find Tenants Easily?

Looking at the broader picture, keep in mind that not every house—and not every neighborhood—lends itself to having tenants. You should think twice about a conversion if apartments in houses are a rarity where you are because there are dozens of new, or fairly new, rental complexes in town, with units carrying all the bells and whistles. Most folks will gravitate toward them. You will be competing with built-in microwave ovens, central air conditioning, new or almost new wall-to-wall carpeting, half a bath more than you have to offer, and let's not forget a pool and/or tennis court. Oh, and a clubhouse, too, which you most certainly do not have. And maybe a covered parking space. You will have a hard time finding tenants unless you are offering rents substantially lower than those of the showier new communities.

Or unless you are in an old-house neighborhood, perhaps one in a historic district. Those homes offer handsome features not likely to be found in newer, cookie-cutter communities, such as mouldings, parquet floors, medallion ceilings, marble mantels and the like. Those addresses are likely to be choice, drawing tenants who prefer a home with "character." You should do well renting in such an area.

Keep zoning in mind if you live in a preservation area, though. You might be allowed to create apartments—the houses in your neighborhood are probably too large for today's smaller families, a fact the zoning board is likely to acknowledge—but in most instances you will be confined to altering the interior while keeping the exterior of your home looking pretty much the way it does now. That means no separate entrance carved into the outside of the dwelling. So if your zoning board says yes to a conversion, check to see if there is also a landmarks commission where you are, and what rules that body has laid down for the streets it oversees.

Creating a Rental Apartment

Once you have your permissions, you can make that rental unit out of any part of the house you choose. Perhaps the basement is an obvious choice. It may already have a bath, and will need only a small kitchen (it will have to have adequate daylight, and you will also have to be sure there is no danger from radon if that is a problem in your part of the country. If it is, look in the Yellow Pages of your telephone book under "Radon Testing Services" to have your home checked). You might also consider converting a wing of your house, or the top floor, or any other configuration you think will work.

Logue says there is a large Victorian home down the street from her, a three-story wood frame house that was separated *vertically* into two full units. Each tenant has three floors to himself or herself. The front door looks like others in the neighborhood, but once inside there are two more entries, each opening to that tenant's living room. These days no one in Logue's neighborhood recalls why the home-owner carved up the house in that particular fashion, but it works. So you don't automatically have to think in terms of horizontal units.

Do not assume you will need a separate bedroom for the unit either. There is certainly a market for small but attractive studio apartments. You might have an eat-in kitchen in *your* apartment, but a much smaller kitchen with no tables and chairs and a compact refrigerator that fits under a counter can be just fine with some renters (as long as there is room for a microwave oven!).

Ask yourself, too, as you consider this project: Who is my likely tenant? Am I near the commuter bus line, or the subway stop? Can I offer parking space? Is my house within walking distance of a college or university? Each of your perks can translate into a slightly higher rent than that asked by those in your community who answer no to those questions. At the least it can mean renting your place before the ones that have less to offer.

Nose around a little, too, while you are thinking about conversion. Talk to real estate agents. What is the rental situation like in your town? Too many apartments with not enough renters? Is it tight, with any new unit coming on the market likely to be snapped right up?

Be sure your tenant's unit is as nice as you can make it, for the obvious reason that the more attractive it is, the more you can charge to live there.

Naturally, the unglamorous electrical, heating and cooling, and plumbing systems should be in good working order. But then comes what is known as "charming it up," which means doing as much as you can cosmetically for the smallest investment on your part. It is interesting what some low-cost improvements can do to zip up a rather prosaic apartment in an ordinary-looking house. You can, for example, buy a mantel for the living room, even if there is no fireplace (the opening can be filled with dried flowers or some other arrangement of the tenant's choice). If there is a particularly dark area likely to turn off apartment hunters, install a skylight in that hallway or room. The thousand dollars it is likely to cost you will pay itself off soon, since you will not have to give the apartment away because of that fatal flaw.

If you have hardwood floors, have them sanded. That is a more popular look than wall-to-wall carpeting these days, and certainly a smaller outlay of cash on your part.

White is the preferred color for walls. If you are papering over an existing covered wall, opt for a neutral tone and print.

We've talked about entrances. Because of zoning restrictions in your community, you might have to keep the outside of your home intact, and create an interior separation between units. Or, if the house is so constructed, you might be faced with no private stairway for the tenant. He or she will have to troop up to a top floor apartment using *your* interior stairway. This is often done, especially in brownstones and elderly wood-frame houses, while the owners wait for the funds to create an inside entry exclusively for the tenant. It might work best with a student, or with someone who might be paying a lower rent in exchange for babysitting your kids.

The Rent You Will Charge

How much? How high? Four figures, maybe? You will ask, of course, as much as the market will bear. You can check the classified advertisements in your local papers for an idea of what other owners in your town are charging for similar apartments. Remember the variables, however. Apartment A may not sound as nice as yours, but perhaps it is only a block from the grade school, while yours is near no school, bus stop or cluster of stores. Or maybe your block is so-so, while the advertised one was featured in a house tour last year.

By all means talk to some local real estate salespeople about rents. You are under no obligation to sign with any agent. Most will chat with you as a service, hoping to secure your rental unit as their listing, and perhaps your house when you decide to move. So it pays them to be nice.

The Tenant Hunt

- Apartment hunters pay real estate offices a fee, usually a month's rent, for finding them a flat, so there is no charge to you as a landlord.

- Be very sure your realty associate checks a would-be renter's references. Some are in a hurry to conclude a deal and do not bother. You will especially want to know if John Doe is employed where he says he is, at the salary he earns, so the rent is affordable for him. Past landlords' references? You might check, but keep in mind no landlord eager to get rid of a problem tenant is going to tell you anything but what you want to hear: this tenant was a jewel. You will probably do better checking work and bank references.
- There are services like Tenant Chek that can run screenings on prospective tenants to take some of the guesswork out of your interviewing. Tenant Chek (800-922-2214) contacts previous landlords (as mentioned, not always helpful), and also verifies employment and runs credit checks for the applicant you are considering. This costs you a $95 one-time membership fee, plus $25 per tenant screening. They offer more services, such as guarantees on tenants in some situations.
- Whether meeting a tenant in answer to your own advertisement or a prospect brought to you by a realty office, look and listen carefully. Then, armed with as much data as you can secure, go with your instincts. If you don't *like* Bob Bigmouth, don't give him the apartment. (You know, of course, that discrimination on a variety of grounds is against the law. Call your state's department of community affairs for printed material they offer for landlords, which includes antidiscrimination laws.)
- Look into rent control laws in your community, if there are any. In Claudia Logue's city, there are restrictions, but landlords of owner-occupied houses of three units or less have more leeway in various aspects of renting than those with more units, who are considered landlords in the way the owner of the largest complex in the area is considered a landlord. When Logue's apartment becomes vacant she can raise the rent for the next renter more than the small annual percentage allowed by rent control laws, although there is still a lid on that increase.
- Before you start interviewing prospective tenants, have in mind what you want their rent to cover. Will the tenant have to pay his or her own utility bill? Does the house have separate meters for each apartment, or are you both on a master meter? If you will have to pay the entire heating bill, while the tenant picks up

his or her gas and electric charge, that should be calculated into the rent you charge.

- You know how popular pets are in this country? Hey, you say, I have two cats myself. Then do not be too hasty to ban pets in your rental unit. You will eliminate too many good prospects. Claudia Logue has had a succession of four tenants in her duplex over the last seven or eight years. Three came with pets. "I have a dog," she explained. "I was saying no pets for a while at the start, but then there were just too many people calling who did have cats or dogs. I decided to ask for a $100 pet deposit, in the event of damages. It was returned with their security money if everything was all right when they left. I never had to keep that pet deposit."

- Speaking of security deposits, ask around to see what the going charge is in your area. One month's rent is common, a month and a half is becoming more popular, and two months would be even better if you are allowed to ask for that amount. That is separate from a pet deposit, of course.

- Should you offer your tenants a lease? In some communities the small landlord would laugh and say, "Are you kidding?" In others it is customary.

  It's wiser to go with a lease. You can buy a standard lease in any stationery store. Quite frankly, they are written by owners' groups, so they are slanted in your favor. Be sure to fill in blank spaces where you want to note a pet deposit, or whether the tenant is to maintain the lawn, or whatever other special stipulation you are making with your rental of the apartment.

The Seasonal Landlord

Is your primary residence in a resort area? Good for you. Look into creating a rental apartment that you can lease for big bucks in season, and might even be able to let to a student for the school year (assuming summer is high season where you are), so it will be vacant from Memorial Day to Labor Day.

Bedside Reading

Consumer magazines geared at managing finances, such as *Money, Kiplinger's Personal Finance* magazine and others, frequently print articles on the advantages of the two-family house. Check your library's copy of the *Reader's Guide to Periodical Literature* to see when such pieces have recently been published. Your library probably has or can get copies of those issues.

The Landlord's Troubleshooter, by Robert Irwin (Dearborn Financial Publishing, 1994, $14.95) is invaluable for the small landlord. It offers solutions to dozens of problems all landlords eventually encounter.

SUMMING UP

$ Check to see if zoning laws prohibit you from having a rental unit in your house.

$ Acquaint yourself with local rental regulations, such as rent control laws.

$ Check would-be tenants' references.

$ Have your new rental unit looking good, and running smoothly, as quickly as you can. Both will help with a quick rental, and will also relieve you of an immediate rush of phone calls from your new tenants about repairs, replacements, and so on.

$ Be responsible, and responsive to tenants' legitimate complaints.

CHAPTER 8

A Day Care Center in Your Home

What follows seems an appropriate reminiscence to kick off this chapter. The scene is a small town near Philadelphia, the year 1984.

"I was working and loved my job, but then I had a baby," Patricia C. ("Trisha") Gallagher recalls of that time. "I had a second baby within 18 months. When I told my mother, 'I'm going to look for a babysitter for both kids,' she said, 'You're not going back to work with two children, are you?' I said, 'Oh no, Mom, I'm just going to do something from home.'

"So I called the Small Business Administration. I was quite proud of myself. I said, 'I have an MBA, I've been an account executive at AT&T and I was wondering what I could do from home.' I thought the guy was going to say, 'Overseas' investment counselor from your kitchen, with your briefcase and your suit,' but he said, 'Lady, why don't you babysit.'"

So she did. Gallagher started a day care center in her home for six children, running it for four years.

She had no trouble initially finding moms to sign up their tots, she says today, "but within the first week five mothers came to me and said they were taking their kids out of my program. I thought, Did I give them yogurt when they were supposed to have baby food? Did my kid bite them? Did *I* bite them?"

The reason for the withdrawals? "They thought it looked like so much fun, they wanted to do it too. They said, 'Oh, she has six kids times $75 a week, she's making a killing. She can just wear jogging suits, we have to get dressed up. We have expensive lunches, she has peanut butter and jelly with the kids and saves money.'"

Sound familiar? Are you Trisha Gallagher, or are you one of the moms who can almost instantly spot an entrepreneurial opportunity?

Day care is certainly needed in this country, at all levels of a child's growth. Home businesses in general continue to open at a regular clip, by enterprising Americans convinced they can make their product or service invaluable to the consumer. Put the two together, and the result is moms can have successful careers as child center owners, allowing them to stay home, perhaps with their own infants or toddlers, and earn a nice bit of money too.

Can *you* pull this off? It's very likely you *can*. This can be a very profitable home-based business, and one you can enjoy as well.

What's Involved Here

Before you consider licensing, marketing and the myriad other details attached to opening any business, give serious thought to how you will manage a houseful of babies or preschoolers.

If you are at home now with your own small child (or two), how many more do you think you can comfortably manage? One? Three? Remember, the key here is to run the center yourself, without a "staff," which in several respects ushers you into a whole other category as far as how the government views your enterprise. You might start small, taking in one child and growing as your confidence does.

If you have no small children at home, and indeed have not had for quite some time, it is even more important to start with one infant or tot, to see how much time you can spare to include one more, and then another.

Regulating authorities will probably put the ceiling on in-home care at about six children, although rules and restrictions in this area vary across the country and change regularly. If you want to expand beyond that number, you will have to become a commercial day care center, which calls for a different licensing procedure.

Trisha Gallagher did that, too, when she expanded her operation to tend 11 children and ran *that* program for four years. Gallagher so immersed herself in child care that she wrote two books on the subject for would-be operators. These days her work hours are filled with lectures, writing, offering workshops and consulting on the subject. She now has four children, ranging in age from 11 to four.

Back to *your* business. Another point to consider in your can-I-really-do-this musing: the folks who live with you. "In order to start any type of business from home you should have the support of your family," Gallagher points out. Talk to your family, painting a realistic picture of what is likely to happen around your place if it becomes a small day care center.

You will need someone as backup in the event you become ill, too. That can be your mom, or your sister or a friend, whom you will probably pay for helping out. That individual must be able to step in, perhaps on short notice, when you simply cannot take in your charges, but do not want to inconvenience their parents and possibly jeopardize your business by "calling in sick."

You will have to think about what you can offer the children in your care. Infants, when they are not napping, can be easily amused. Toddlers—well, now you really have to look deep within yourself. No parent is going to want his or her child plopped in front of a television set all day while you do household chores, no matter how many terrific kiddie videos you are willing to buy or rent.

"What will be expected here," Gallagher explains, "depends on the standards the parents have for care. Most people want their kids to learn colors and numbers. There are games you can play for these instructions, and even some that exercise all parts of the body. All of this will be interesting for you as a provider. It keeps you motivated. It's nice to have a routine, activities that even you look forward to."

So you will have to spend preparation time putting together a curriculum of sorts, so you can tell parents what you have to offer that will make your center special.

Consider your hours A home day care operation can run from 6:30 AM to 7 PM, or later. Perhaps you are more interested in an after-school program—picking up a few small kids from school, maybe kindergarten, and bringing them back to your house until their parents call for them.

Is there any personality type that should not consider day care? Gallagher says women who are overly fastidious about their homes, since there will be a fair amount of wear and tear here. Those who are not flexible will find day care frustrating. Gallagher adds, "You have to be able to love other people's children." Is that a quality you can bring to this business?

Finally, there is your home to consider. Is it roomy enough for a few more people, even small ones? If not, can you create the illusion of space, or at least of not being crowded? Susan Bernstein ran a home-based day care center for a while from her New Jersey two-bedroom apartment, but concedes quite a few would-be customers did not sign up with her when they saw she had no yard. Also, she adds, while she has had parties at her place with several dozen guests, and was using one bedroom for a playroom, again, moms had the impression her space was too small.

"It was hard getting started," says Bernstein, who holds a degree in early childhood education and has since returned to a paying position in that field. "But at times I had as many as five children at once, and no parent complained once her child was enrolled." Bernstein's hours were 8 AM to 6 PM, and she charged "over $100 a week."

Becoming Licensed

Call your local office of your state's department of health and rehabilitative services. If that office does not regulate home day care, people there can refer you to the agency that does. Once you have the right office and person on the phone, that individual can advise you of neighborhood zoning restrictions, if any, to home-based businesses exactly where you are. If their answer to you is "no way," then that is the end of your fledgling concept, at least as far as keeping the business at home. You can certainly weigh setting up a center away from your place and elsewhere in town. You might look into the possibility of securing a variance to a restrictive law, although that is not always successful. Many residential neighborhoods frown on businesses operated from home, and residents simply will not be swayed. Of course, your neighbors' okaying your proposal can be an important part of your winning a variance.

You might have another hurdle to cross. Perhaps you live in a community or housing development bound by an association's rules, and there it is in black and white in the bylaws: "Businesses operated out of the home are not permitted." Can you go ahead anyway, hoping no one will find out? You can—and they will. The cars and children coming and going early in the morning and late in the afternoon will not help keep your secret. You will have to ask your association's board of directors for permission after the fact, and will have to dismantle your program if the answer is a firm no. It's better to ask before buying the cutouts and crepe paper.

Once you get the green light from all with something to say about your venture, the office that oversees day care in your area (which will be your continuing contact throughout your days in this business) will advise you of the next steps. One is having your home checked for a reasonable degree of cleanliness and for obvious hazards. An inspector will look for a fire extinguisher in the kitchen, smoke alarms, outlet covers, poisonous substances away from the reach of toddlers and so forth. You will also probably be required to pass a physical examination (to see if you are carrying any contagious diseases, not to check your stamina!), and your background will be checked to see if you have a criminal record. Fingerprinting might be called for in some states.

Once you are in operation, you will be visited periodically to see that you are continuing to meet that agency's standards.

A few communities require their day care owners to complete a short course, offered by those agencies or participating educational institutions. That might be a daylong workshop on various aspects of child care in the home, including educational games and activities.

Start-up Costs

They are minimal.

You will likely have to pay $25 or so for a permit or license for your center.

Check your homeowners insurance policy, and talk with your agent about extended coverage for this business. You will probably need a rider to your existing policy, at a cost of perhaps $300 a year. Trisha Gallagher says to count on spending roughly $50 per child.

There is no need to buy any new furniture at first. As your center grows you might spring for kiddie tables and chairs, or other furniture. If you have small children at home, you probably have enough toys to start, although you will probably want to buy some inexpensive educational materials.

You might not have to spend one dime to advertise your service. Day care providers usually find their own neighborhood offers a sizable pool of likely enrollees. Announcing your new business in a community newsletter, or one published by your house of worship, is likely to be free or at a minimal cost and may bring you all the business you need. Some local or state regulatory agencies keep a file of approved day care centers, and you might secure some referrals from that source.

You might want to have a contract printed spelling out your terms for this service, such as drop-off and pick-up times for the children, payment due just before the week coming up (to avoid payment problems, which some owners say can be a genuine concern), whether your business will be open on holidays and how you will handle sick children. On the latter point, you might want a signed consent form for medical treatment of a child in your care if he or she is hospitalized in an emergency.

Setting a Price

How much to charge for all this? Whatever the market will bear. Trisha Gallagher suggests calling day care centers in your community to get an idea of the range of rates, which, with different centers offering different programs, is likely to be broad. Generally, parents pay anywhere from $50 to more than $100 for care in someone's home. The average price hovers at around $100 a week.

Rates for infants can be $10 or so higher than for toddlers.

Expenses

Let's say you tend three toddlers at $100 a week for 50 weeks, for a gross annual income of $15,000. You will pay income taxes on that amount, of course, and make your own Social Security contribution, since you are self-employed. But your expenses can help defray taxes. A part of your house will be deductible as a business expense. That rider to your homeowners insurance policy is deductible. The $2,000 or so a year you spend for lunches and snacks for the kids is another deduction. So is the $250 for art supplies and games. And the $75 a day you paid your sister-in-law for taking over for you those four days in February when you were ill. And so on.

Need To Know More?

You probably do, and firsthand, too. You might contact a child care provider or two in your community, to ask the many questions you no doubt have. Someone who already has enough kids enrolled is not likely to be in competition with your new business, and could be very generous with guidance. You might even be able to spend a morning there to see how a typical day goes. Ask what you should do differently when you start up. What are that care provider's biggest concerns? And, of course, what does that person charge?

There is reading material that can help you as well. *Start Your Own At-Home Child Care Business* by Patricia C. Gallagher, updated in 1994, costs $19.95 and is for the smaller business. *So You Want to Open a Profitable Day Care Center*, also by Gallagher and also in a 1994 edition, costs $19.95 and is geared toward the individual looking to start a larger day care establishment. Write Young Sparrow Press, Box 555, Worcester, PA 19490, or call 215-364-1945.

"How to Start a Good Early Childhood Program" is a free brochure available from the National Association for the Education of Young Children. Write NAEYC Information Service, 1509 Sixteenth St. NW, Washington, DC 20036.

SUMMING UP

$ Be sure you have family support for your business.

$ Know yourself well enough to know this is work you can do—and do well.

$ Follow local regulation of this industry.

$ Start small.

$ Plan well, to keep kids interested, amused and learning.

$ Talk to as many day care owners, and workers, as you can where you live.

CHAPTER 9

Making Small
Repairs Yourself

The bathroom drain is clogged. The screen door needs replacing. You bought bookshelves, but they have to be secured to the wall. The trees out front and back ought to be trimmed. Oh, and you just noticed yesterday. . .

Do you know how much all of that will cost if farmed out to professionals? You say you do because that's how you get most repairs or improvements made at your place?

You must want to save a few dollars, even in this area of home-owning, or you would not have this book and would not be reading this chapter.

So perhaps it is time to knuckle down to doing small repairs yourself. The big stuff? Sure, spring for a professional to replace the roof. And you probably will not want to install wall-to-wall carpeting yourself. But the kind of jobs that take an electrician, plumber or handyman 15 to 20 minutes to fix but cost you $50 or more for labor can certainly be done by a newly trained do-it-yourselfer, right? That's the spirit.

What's Involved Here

Obviously you're going to have to learn a few things about home repair. Not too much, just enough. Again, we are not talking about building an addition to your house, just fixing the niggling little on-the-fritz whatnots that crop up around any home.

"Making repairs yourself saves time, money and is a source of satisfaction," says Robert Berko. Berko is executive director of Consumer Education Research Center, a national nonprofit consumer organization founded in 1969. He is also the author of *Small Home Repairs Made Easy* ($5.95 plus $2 postage and handling, available from the Consumer Center, 350 Scotland Road, Orange, NJ 07050 or by calling 800-872-0121 with a credit card).

"It may seem daunting at first to do a particular job," Berko continues, "but when it's broken down to small steps, it's not that hard."

We've talked about money as a motivation for doing it yourself, but Berko, who was the head of one of the state's largest home improvement contracting companies, raises another valid point for picking up your own hammer.

"One of the main things here," he explains, "is not whether you can do something yourself, but whether you can *get* somebody to do it for you. It's hard to find anyone to come to your home for a bill of less than four or five figures these days. They don't want the job."

Berko says even the most unskilled among us can unstop a toilet, fix the doorbell and repair the garage door. And more.

Fear and Loathing

Many of us do not make even the simplest repairs around our place because we are not interested enough to bother (until now) or are afraid we will hurt ourselves or bring down the house—literally. Making electrical repairs seems to be the biggest fear of all.

Doug Tarencz now makes most routine repairs around his New Jersey home, after completing construction of a wing to the house he built with just one worker helping him. He had no particular interest in puttering before the purchase of a too-small home in a highly desirable neighborhood led him to a major remodeling project (more about that in Chapter 1).

"Most people are extremely uncomfortable dealing with electricity," he says. "But as long as you follow the directions—in a book or whatever you're reading—you don't have to be afraid. Actually, I enjoy doing electrical work more than any other kind." (Naturally when you attack these repairs, you will be sure the appliance is unplugged or, on house wiring, that the fuse has been unscrewed or the circuit breaker tripped, cutting off power.)

Tarencz's last three "small jobs" around the house that he says any beginner can do: putting in a bi-fold door, rewiring a lamp and replacing a toilet. "That's not hard," he says of the latter installation. "It only looks hard."

Learning How To

You say you can see Tarencz's point, but your talents really do lie elsewhere. How can I fix something when I'm not even sure exactly what's wrong, you ask. Don't you have to be a *little* into this?

Good questions. But you are not in this alone. There are many services and people out there eager to help you, even to pointing out exactly where the problem is if you have no idea why something is not working properly. Some have made a multimillion dollar business assisting and encouraging do-it-yourselfers.

- First, and perhaps simplest, you can ask a family member or good friend who is handy, to help you with a small job. You can learn from him or her and then continue on your own, or at least know how to do it next time.

  Jennie Mumola, who lives on the East Coast, has helped so many family members and friends wallpaper she can hardly keep track of them all: Her daughter and son-in-law. Her son and daughter-in-law. A woman who worked in her husband's office. And so on.

  "I don't charge anybody," she says. "You can save a lot of money doing wallpapering yourself." Sometimes Mumola does the entire job; sometimes she simply "starts" whomever she is helping, and that person completes the project.

  "It looks so nice when it's finished," she adds, "and you feel like you've really helped somebody."
- Next is a familiar path to learning. Collect magazine and newspaper articles on specific home repairs, many of which are written in detail and illustrated. You can have quite a file in no time, and can use those instructions as you need them.

- In the same vein, there are any number of books you can buy—Robert Berko's, for example—to guide you through small repairs. Some are simplified, with the sort of "home repairs for dummies who hammer their thumbs" theme. One, or even a collection, of those volumes can repay you their cost with just a couple of service calls you will not have to make.

  For Tarencz, the purchase 15 years ago of the *Reader's Digest Complete Do-It-Yourself Manual* has seen him through dozens of small repairs to the two New Jersey homes he has owned over those years. The book, he explains, "has been my bible, although I hardly look at it now because I've outgrown it."

- Since most of what breaks or malfunctions requires your buying something to fix it, turn to the people at the hardware store for assistance. When you buy the widget you need, they can tell you how to install it. Better yet, you can just tell how something or other is not working correctly. They can direct you to what you need to fix it, and then tell you how to use it.

- Home centers, which have sprung up over the last decade or so, make it their mission to guide homeowners and small contractors through every aspect of home improvements and repairs. They offer courses and workshops throughout the year on a variety of subjects—wallpapering, painting and laying tile are just a few. Next time you are in the one nearest you, look at the bulletin board to see just how many opportunities they provide for hands-on training in home repairs and improvements.

- Adult education programs at community colleges, and evening adult classes in high schools can also help the novice. A course titled "Home Repairs for Beginners" can cost as little as $10 or $25 and can not only start you on the road to fixing your house yourself, but also can offer you an almost personal tutor in the form of your teacher. Bring your problems and questions to class!

- Is an appliance not working? Before calling in someone, or taking it someplace—you will be handed a bill in either event—look for the materials that came with the gizmo when you bought it. Most have directions for making simple repairs. Also, most major companies like Whirlpool, General Electric and the like usually have toll-free numbers that customers can call for help with products that do not work. Those folks can often diagnose the problem and tell you how to fix the item so you don't have to call in a professional. You might also call your local manufacturer's representative about repairs. You may be surprised to learn they might not be all that eager to come out on a service call. Most have a checklist to run through with the consumer, and often can help over the phone, at no charge at all.

If you have not kept the printed material that came with your appliance, call the manufacturer. Besides a telephone hot line, most offer booklets that can pinpoint problems and offer solutions. Maytag, for example, will send the 13-page booklet "Before You Call . . .," which goes into likely problems and solutions to appliance repair. To obtain a copy, send 50 cents in coins to Maytag Company, Consumer Information Center, Dept. 206YG, Newton, IA 50208.

Whirlpool offers the booklet "Nice Things To Know About . . . Preventing Appliance Service Calls." It is free from Whirlpool Corporation, Appliance Information Service, PO Box 405, St. Joseph, MO 49085.

Incidentally, manufacturers say the most common mistakes made by users are: washers not properly plugged in, dryers that take too long to dry because the lint filter needs cleaning, dishwashers not cleaning properly because the home hot water heater isn't set hot enough and refrigerator temperature controls turned to off.

- If you still feel more comfortable having a professional over for a repair, look closely at how he or she does the job, so you may be able to do it yourself next time. Ask questions along the lines of "So what does looping that around there do?" rather than "If I want to do this myself . . ."

- Tools can be costly, especially if you are new to doing it yourself and have to start from scratch. Some communities have "tool libraries," under the auspices of a local community development agency or a similar government office operating locally.

To save money on some power tools used infrequently, Sandra M. Brassfield, a Seattle rehabber of dozens of properties and author of "Profiting From Real Estate Rehab" (John Wiley & Sons, Inc., 1992, $19.95), suggests you form a tool library with relatives, nearby friends or neighbors. Buy the power tools you all agree on, perhaps one at a time. It's highly unlikely everyone is going to need the same tool at the same time.

One problem with this, Brassfield concedes, is "some people feel strongly about tools, so maybe buying within a family is better. Relatives who belong can even make contributions to the tool library with holiday gifts."

Still another idea: Rent the tools you need instead of buying. You can rent infrequently used floor polishers, airless paint sprayers, carpet cleaners, floor strippers and a variety of other gizmos and heavy-duty machinery, at prices that are just a small percentage of the purchase price.

One more tip in this area. Wait and bunch repairs in one area—plumbing, electricity, etc.—together before calling in a professional if there is no emergency and you cannot do the job yourself. You will pay just one service call charge instead of two or three.

How Maintenance Saves Money

Just as the best health care is said to be prevention, the best way to cope with home repairs is to avoid a good chunk of them through maintenance.

To keep up with what needs to be done on a regular—although perhaps only annual—basis around your home, you can buy a book that will take you through maintenance, with a smattering of repairs where needed, on a seasonal basis. *The New York Times Season-by-Season Guide to Home Maintenance* by John Warde (Times Books, 1992, $25.00) might be your choice. *Better Homes and Gardens Complete Guide to Home Repair, Maintenance and Improvement* by the magazine's staff (Meredith Corp., 1980, $24.95) is another in this area. Both are heavily illustrated.

SUMMING UP

$ Service calls for home repairs are costly. Try to do as many as you can on your own.

$ There are many sources of help for the novice do-it-yourselfer.

$ A common reason for appliances not working is that they are not plugged in, a good reason for calling the manufacturer's hot line before calling a serviceperson!

$ Regular home maintenance can avert a number of repair and replacement problems.

CHAPTER 10

50 Ways
To Save on
Utility Bills

Is a member of your household constantly after you to turn off the lights, reminding you to shut the front door or tsk-tsking about some other venial sin you are committing against energy conservation?

Do you watch local television news segments about energy efficiency and, when hearing valuable suggestions, say, "Gee, I have to remember that"? And then you don't?

Do the energy-saving tips your utility company sends with your monthly bill end up in the trash because you have eyes only for the amount you owe?

Here is a chapter to make you feel absolutely virtuous about saving money by using less heat, air-conditioning, electricity and water—if you adopt most of its suggestions.

What follows are 50 tips, all in one place and in writing. Almost certainly included in this list are the bits from newspaper items you have saved but are now misplaced and probably most of the other advice you have heard all your life about saving energy.

Part of the problem in home energy conservation is that one lone suggestion picked up here and there seems like it will save only pennies. And so you think "Eh, big deal," right? But seeing those pennies add up as you make your way through the list that follows will show that we all waste an appreciable sum of money daily through thoughtlessness or lack of information about conserving energy.

And then there is this: you can hold on to far more than pennies in this area. As you read on, you will see that some utilities around the country offer rebates on certain appliance purchases and low-interest loan programs for some major installations such as storm windows. Now we're talking more sizable savings!

What's Involved Here

This will require attention to detail on your part, sticking with the project even when you think you are nickel-and-diming yourself to death. You might also have to make a few inexpensive purchases and installations.

Another point here, and a good-news one: besides the savings that will go into your pocket making these changes, they will benefit you when you decide to sell your home. Energy conservation is in, as is any kind of saving these days, and the house that has already been updated will look very attractive to prospective buyers. This is not a vitally important home improvement, of course—it's not a new *roof*—but the changes you make in this area show the attention you have paid to your home over the years. That is noticeable to house-hunters, and very appealing. No one wants to believe their next home has not been cared for.

The utilities in your area and your state are only too happy to offer as much as they can to help customers conserve. Really. First, it's good public relations for them. Second, as you have seen in summertime brownouts and occasional water main breaks in older cities, many utility companies must consider expansion of their facilities and services, which is a very expensive proposition. If they can get customers to accept incentives for savings and conservation, they can delay those costly plans for a while longer.

Pull out one old gas or electric bill and a water bill, selecting each for the same month—a month when usage is about average, not high with summer or winter usage. Use these for the baseline bill. Wait a couple of months after making some changes around your place, and then match those bills up with a current one. All things being equal, you should receive a nice surprise at the difference between the two. Unless you have been terribly profligate with energy, it will not be $100 or more that you have saved. But over the year it can run into three figures, and perhaps more. It's better to have that money in *your* pocket than the utility companies'.

So here we go.

50 Ways To Save

Heating, Cooling and Electric Bills

1. For an inexpensive alternative to a home security system, turn on the porch light at night. This can be done automatically when you are away in the same way you use timers to turn on lights inside your home to reduce the chances of a break-in.
2. Check windows, window frames and doors for heating or cooling leaks.
3. A familiar caution: close doors to the outside quickly, so heat or air-conditioning does not escape. Our parents were right with their constant, "Close the door, we don't love Con Ed" (or Public Service, or whomever).
4. Storm windows, besides working to keep heat inside your home, are another asset when the time comes to sell.
5. If you are thinking of making an energy-saving improvement, such as those storm windows, or perhaps insulation, contact your local utility company to see if it offers a low-cost loan program for those upgrades. Many do, at favorable rates to homeowners.
6. Ask your utility company what it offers in guidance for those purchases. Even if the company has no loan program, it is in a position to steer you toward solid products, and away from those that will not work well for you.
7. Sometime during the year, ask your utility company to send someone to your home for a free home-energy check. This can be invaluable, since you have an individual looking personally at all the money wasters in your home. These home-energy checks should be distinguished from a heating or cooling checkup, which can be free from your utility at certain times of the year but cost $10 or so just before peak usage times.
8. Speaking of your heating or cooling system, call a qualified service specialist to check yours annually for maximum effi-

ciency and to prevent breakdowns during major hot spells or cold snaps.

9. Install ceiling fans, so you can keep rooms cool but use your air-conditioner less.

10. Raising your thermostat is an effective way to lower summer cooling bills. The recommended setting for normal usage is 78 degrees, with the fan set on AUTO.

11. It is a fallacy, but a commonly held perception, that it costs you more if you turn off air conditioning when you go out than if you simply let it run. If you are going to be out a couple of hours, turn off the system.

12. Expecting a hot summer? Or is that redundant where you are? Two tips: Plant some trees, if you can, on the south and west sides of your home. Also, keep shades and draperies drawn during the hottest part of the day. Awnings also provide shade (canvas is in, aluminum is out). All of the above will save on air-conditioning consumption.

13. Here's something to write for: "How to Keep Your Cool and Save Cold Cash" is free when you send a business-sized envelope with two first-class stamps on it to the Air Conditioning and Refrigeration Institute, 4301 N. Fairfax Dr., Suite 425, Arlington, VA 22203.

14. Use the sun to your advantage in the winter by opening draperies and raising shades to let in daylight warmth and keeping them closed at night.

15. Weatherstripping around doors and caulking around window frames will keep warm air inside your home and cold air out.

16. Insulate your attic or top-floor ceiling. A reputable insulation dealer in your community can bring you up-to-date on today's standards and selections, based on the climate in your part of the country.

17. Your thermostat should be away from lamps or other lighting, which may cause your system to operate excessively.

18. Change furnace filters regularly. Dirty filters impede air flow, making your system work harder and longer. A reminder: change the filter once a month, when you are paying your utility bill.

19. Circulating fans, mentioned above as a coolant, also can keep rooms warm in the winter.

20. How do you heat your home? It might pay to see if other systems are less costly to run (you may already know they are!). It will cost to make a change, of course, but if you plan to stay in that house for several years, it will pay you back eventually.

21. If you have an outside heating or cooling plant, be sure it is kept clear of leaves and other debris.

22. When running kitchen and bathroom ventilating fans, shut them off quickly. Utility companies say those fans can blow away a household of warm (or cool) air in just one hour!

23. Building a new home? Your local utility company can offer information on energy-saving devices that can be installed during the building process. The Public Service Company of Colorado, for example, offers a brochure titled "Buying an Ideal Energy Home," a guide to building energy efficiency into the home as it is going up. Many utility companies also offer free workshops for the new-home builder (or homebuyer). If you are not building, but want to incorporate some of the company's suggestions into your home now, call and see how strict it is about the must-be-building stipulation in its advertisement.

24. Turn off your furnace pilot light during the summer, but check first with your gas company.

25. If your home does not have them, install vents on the roof to keep the attic or crawl space from trapping heat, which then costs you money to cool.

26. Are you wasting light—and money—in some spaces? Do you really need a 100-watt light bulb in a hallway? Does anyone *read* there? Or 100 watts in the garage? If you have a workshop there, you can have more light at that work area without having to illuminate the entire garage space.

27. Have some gloomy spots around your house? A hallway? A bath with no windows? Install a skylight. The light from a skylight reduces the amount of artificial lighting you will need and, perhaps equally important, will make your home more attractive come resale time because the dark corners are gone.

28. Replace some lighting fixtures with fluorescent lights if you can. A 25-watt fluorescent provides light equal to a 100-watt incandescent. Yes, we all look dreadful in artificial light, but

if it is over the kitchen sink, or in similar no-nonsense spots, who cares?

29. Surge protectors are an inexpensive way to protect your televisions, VCRs and personal computer from lightning surges or power outages. They do not save energy or lower your electric bill, but are mentioned here because some folks think they do.

Appliances

30. Did you know that chest-style freezers are 10 to 15 percent more energy efficient than uprights?

31. Front-load washing machines use about one-third less water than top-load models. If the dishwasher you buy has a built-in heater, it will let you keep your hot water thermostat lower.

32. Keep the lint screen in your clothes dryer clean, a common failing of many homeowners. The lint impedes the flow of air into the dryer, causing the machine to consume more energy.

33. Natural gas appliances cost less to operate than those fueled by electricity or propane.

34. Look for energy ratings when buying these big-ticket items.

35. If you are shopping for a major appliance, ask if your utility company offers partial rebates on those purchases. Some do, if the buyers follow certain guidelines.

36. Use microwave ovens and pressure cookers if you have them. They save energy and reduce cooking time.

37. Keep an eye out for pamphlets offered by appliance manufacturers that can save you money. You can, for example, write for a copy of "Energy-Saving Tips," offered by Maytag. The 16-page booklet offers a number of tips, including a section on energy guide labels, required by law on all new U.S. washers, dishwashers and refrigerators. To get your copy, write to Energy-Saving Tips, Maytag Company, Department 392YG, One Dependability Square, Newton, IA 50208.

Water, Water, Everywhere

38. If your community has restrictions on watering the lawn, by all means obey them. Saving $10 from your quarterly water

bill goes, well, right down the drain if you have to pay a $25 fine for being caught watering when you are not supposed to. Sometimes watering with a hand-held hose is allowed during so called nonwatering times of the day, while using an in-ground watering system is banned. Check your community's regulations.

39. Water lawns and outdoor plants in the morning or evening. You will save water because it evaporates so quickly during the day that you will need more to do the same job.

40. Ask your water company if it has any printed material on the subject of conservation. If it does, those brochures will be aimed specifically at your community and its concerns.

41. Have an automatic irrigation system for your yard? A tip suggested in Chapter 5 bears repeating here. You can buy a water gauge gizmo that will not let your system turn on if there has just been a shower or if your lawn has already received enough water. It costs $10 to $15 at your local home or garden center.

42. Install a low-flow shower head. These $10 gadgets can save you 50 percent on an average shower, which consumes about 35 gallons of water.

43. While you're at it, you can buy a few low-flow aerators to attach to the faucets in your kitchen and baths. Costing about $4 apiece, they cut water flow in half, and combined with the shower savings can slice your water and water-heating bills substantially. These aerators add air to the water and make the curb in water use hardly noticeable.

44. Do not run water while you are brushing your teeth or shaving.

45. Look around for plumbing leaks and have them plugged.

46. Have a problem with a toilet that uses too much water when it is flushed? Something called a flapper (cost: under $10) will keep it from wasting water.

47. There are kits available for insulating your hot water tank and piping. If buying new, opt for a heater with thick insulation around the shell. It might cost more than one with thinner protection, but the energy savings over time will easily make up for that initial outlay.

48. Keep the thermostat on your hot water heater at the lowest possible setting to maintain a comfortable hot water temperature.

49. Use cold water for washing clothes whenever possible.
50. Do you wash your car yourself, at least sometimes? Don't keep the hose running. Use a sponge, with water in a bucket, turning on the hose only for the initial hose-down and then for rinsing.

Questions, Anyone?

If you have questions about your household's energy use, the Energy Efficiency and Renewable Energy Clearinghouse, part of the U.S. Department of Energy, can provide information on a wide range of topics, from passive solar energy to energy-efficient appliances. This office was established in 1994 and combines the services of two other federal agencies. The phone number is 800-363-3732.

SUMMING UP

$ Saving on heating, cooling, electric and water bills can add up to big bucks.

$ The more you do in this area now, the more appealing your home will be when you want to sell

$ Local utility companies offer much in the way of guidance—printed material, home checkups, rebates, even low-cost loans. Call to see what is available where you live.

$ An easy way to keep up-to-date on this subject: read the newsletters that come with your utility company's bills.

CHAPTER 11

Six More Great Ideas for Unused Space at Your Place

If you're not using it, why not let someone else have x number of square feet in or around your home—for a price, of course.

These tips will not work for everyone—they are highly specialized. But some of you reading one or two of them will jump out of your chair with a "yes!" and then, voilá! More cash from the old homestead. And probably some admiration from your neighbors, too, on your ingenuity.

To avoid repeating two important caveats continually throughout this chapter, here they are before we start: Check your local zoning authority to see if you can use your home for the purposes suggested and look into your insurance coverage as well, perhaps calling your agent to clarify anything not spelled out in your policy.

Now let's shake the bushes for still more money from your place.

What's Involved Here

Specifically, it's recognizing a need and setting out to fill it, which is the slogan for any good business or great commercial idea.

Your Garage

To start, take a look at your garage. If you have a two-car structure but own just one automobile, why not clear out the other half of the room and rent it? You would be wise not to rent a one-car garage, however. You'll lose money leaving your car on the street. It will last longer if protected in a garage.

Chelle Delaney handled the renting of her mother's garage, which consists of three units, two of them unused or underused. (We first met Delaney in Chapter 5.)

Delaney rented one unit, which had its own door and a plywood partition to separate it from the other units, to a neighbor who had many items he wanted to store.

"We're now thinking of renting the third space," she says, "to a man who has a classic car and wants to protect it. He wanted to make sure the garage has a concrete floor, which it does. It doesn't have a partition, but he says he'll put up one, which is fine with us."

Delaney, who lives in a mid-sized Southern city, says the space is renting at "under $50 a month." You might be able to command more where you live. Still, that's a nice piece of change for having a tenant and not having to do anything in the way of services!

You might check around at parking lots and garages where you are to see what you can charge for the space you want to rent. Ask a would-be tenant if he or she can make use of some of the storage room (or shelves, if you have them) alongside the wall where the car will be parked. If the answer is yes, factor that into the rent.

Delaney has no written agreement with the tenant for the first unit she rented. She said he paid cash for a full year when he agreed to take the space. You might want a written agreement, however.

A Darkroom

Do you have a darkroom in your home? That might be space you can rent to professional or amateur photographers. Certainly there is a sizable chunk of time during the week when you are not using it, and for a few hours at least someone else might as well be there. Rent by the hour at a fee you can decide by calculating what the market will bear for that sort of space and whether you are offering any developing or other materials along with the room.

Is Your Home on Water?

Do you live on a river, bay or some other body of water that boaters seem to enjoy? If you have a dock, you can rent it. Or you can make it longer and rent part of it. If you have no dock, you can build one for the specific purpose of leasing.

First, be sure there is enough demand for boat slips where you are. For example, in California, Florida and parts of the Northeast, you will probably find a continuing need.

"Where there's a high demand, waterfront property can be a real money-maker," says Anne Johnson, a national boating writer and columnist profiled in Chapter 4.

Johnson adds, "Most owners don't use their boats that often, so if you're worried about being trampled by people in the summer, don't be. Many go out maybe once a month. Some boats have been in one spot for years and haven't moved. Their owners never seem to take them out."

With this, as with the other suggestions, you will have to be sure to consider zoning and insurance regulations. Also, if you live in a community governed by bylaws, check whether your homeowners' association will go along with dock rental. As far as building the dock itself, you will likely have no problem with getting permission. You have a house on a waterway; you are entitled to a dock. If you decide not to use it for your own craft, well. . .

Johnson suggests you also call your state department of natural resources, or whatever that office is called where you are, to determine specific regulations for docks.

Johnson and her husband live on a 40-foot sailboat docked in a large Florida marina and have explored many waterways in this country. She explains if you do not have a dock it will cost several thousand dollars for permits and the construction of one, so be sure there is enough demand for rentals where you are and you can recoup that investment reasonably quickly. If demand is high enough, while you are at it you might want to erect a dock long enough to accommodate several watercraft.

How much money are we talking about earning here? In Fort Lauderdale, Florida, where almost every home has a dock at the end of its yard, rents can run as high as $800 to $900 *per month* in the winter! Bear in mind the area is particularly hopping in the high season with visiting snowbirds needing slips. In other communities, and indeed in Fort Lauderdale in the off-season, rentals are far lower. Where you are, the most you might be able to pull in is $50 to $75 a month.

You will not need a dock at all if the water alongside your property is deep enough. You can make money having a boater park his craft on your lawn, perhaps on a trailer or on blocks. Notes Johnson: "Sometimes we'll be cruising, and we'll see clusters of masts in the distance. Turns out it's hundreds of boats up on solid ground in homeowners' yards."

In setting your rates, you can check area marinas to see what they charge. Keep in mind, however, they are offering services (restrooms, pump-out stations, etc.) that you cannot. So price what you have accordingly.

Another suggestion here: Johnson says some homeowners who have no boat will rent their dock for a low fee in exchange for using that craft and practicing their skills before buying one.

To find a "tenant" or two for your dock, you can run a "Private boat slip" classified advertisement in your local paper.

Extra Storage Space

If you have an empty room in your home and do not want to take in a roomer or housemate, you can offer it as is for storage. More than likely you will have one tenant for the room, but if it is large enough and that individual does not have too many items to store, you might be able to pick up two rent checks.

Before we leave the boating and dock scene, Anne Johnson notes that several houses in the area near her marina rent space in a spare room or attic to boaters. Keep that in mind if your address is very near a waterway.

Have you noticed how popular self-storage warehouses have become over the last couple of decades? It seems no one has enough room to stash everything—and no one seems to want to throw very much out either. The result: a nation of pack rats and an ongoing need for storage.

Do some homework before you offer your room for rent. Look around at area self-storage units. Ask the managers what those warehouses offer in the way of services (climate control, for example); what they charge and what they will not accept for storing (food, for one).

Note how rates are based on the number of square feet of each unit and see how your space compares with those dimensions. You can also ask about hours. Many offer renters 24-hour access to their units. You will not, of course, so take that into account when setting your rate.

What you charge will be based on what you have learned from warehouses and what you offer that they do not. For instance, while your tenants will be able to enter their space only by appointment, you might offer better climate control or better storage for, say, books and files. Clothing, too, might not fare well in a warehouse, but will in a spare bedroom of your house.

You can advertise your space at no charge on area bulletin boards or in local "penny saver" newspapers. If you need to go farther afield than your own neighborhood, run a classified advertisement in your local paper.

A couple of explanations here: the above suggestions relate to what is probably unused space inside your home, on the first or second floors. If you want to rent attic or basement space, you will have to consider the types of items you can store in those areas, given heat, dampness, mildew, bugs and ventilation. The same applies to space in your garage for more than an automobile. A shed is probably worst of all and should be leased only for playground equipment, some sports gear and lawn tools and machinery. Sheds are of flimsier construction than a garage and lack the garage's concrete floor. They have no heat or cooling and are as susceptible to the mildew and bugs of the basement and garage. Don't even think of renting your shed if it leaks when it rains.

An unused bedroom or sewing room is space that is treated like the rest of your home. When it rains, the roof does not leak. When it is hot outdoors, that room is cool. You get the picture.

Board Horses

If you live in "horse country," with plenty of room around your place, consider building a stable on your property and renting it to folks around the area who have a horse but nowhere to keep it. Check around for a fee to charge by calling stables and seeing what they charge and what services they provide.

Sell Off Extra Land

Is your home on a very large lot, perhaps in exurbia? Give some thought to selling off a portion of your land, either to a builder or to a househunter who will buy the land and have a home built there.

Carol and Joe Jensen did just that. The couple bought a small fixer-upper on a two-acre lot. Their plans were to redo the place and sell it quickly. Homes in that area were selling at $150,000 to $200,000.

Then another idea occurred to them.

"We were driving around, and we noticed how much homebuilding was going in that area," Joe Jensen recalls. "And we thought, gee, this house is pretty small and two acres is pretty large. Large enough for another house."

The couple split the lot. They were able to secure a zoning variance that would create two parcels of one acre each.

"We got $9,500 for that lot," Jensen says. "It didn't shortchange the land the house was on, so if you add that to the $36,000 profit we made when we sold the house, we did all right."

This chapter just has to close with what one California man did with his yard. We won't consider these suggestions workable for you, since they are more than a bit outrageous. Of course if you think you can pull it off . . .

A newspaper article ran in newspapers in mid-1994 headlined "Man Turns His Swimming Pool Into Trout Farm in Back Yard." Tired of maintenance, the man had filled his pool with fish. He first made sure the water in the seven-foot-deep pool was free from chlorine and anything else that might hurt a fish. Then he drove to a trout farm and brought home 200 fingerling rainbow trout to stock the pool. He fed the fish daily, and then one fine day invited 100 people over for fishing.

Thus the man emptied his pool before the summer weather warmed the water and killed the fish.

The article concluded with a friend of the man saying that homeowner was full of creative ideas. He had also converted part of his backyard into a professional-quality putting green.

The feature did not mention if the homeowner had charged the fishermen (and women) or the folks using the putting green. If he did, he wins the award for the most creative use of his property.

He becomes our poster boy.

SUMMING UP

$ Don't be too quick to dismiss some of these ideas (aside from the California man's last two). Some folks are making money by implementing them!

$ Check zoning laws and your own homeowners insurance policy before picking up a hammer or placing a classified advertisement.

$ Set your rates carefully. In some instances you may have more to offer than the pros, in others less.

$ If some sort of letter of agreement is common where you are between homeowner and "tenant," draw one up for both you to sign.

PART TWO

For Fun—
And Profit

CHAPTER 12

Running a Bed-and-Breakfast Home

I t is probably a common dream to buy a rambling old house in the country and convert it to a charming bed-and-breakfast inn. It will be great fun to run, and of course wildly profitable.

Well, maybe you don't have to move out of your present home to realize part of that dream. Perhaps you can turn your home into a B&B accommodation and truly enjoy your role as host. Wildly profitable? That does not happen often, even in the country-inn type accommodations. So if you are not going to become rich with this endeavor, you might as well stay in your own home, right?

What's Involved Here

Bed-and-breakfast homes, with roots in Europe, began cropping up here over the last 15 or 20 years. Today there are thousands of accommodations, from the simplest private homes to the most luxurious buildings, structures that could almost be small hotels.

In Europe, B&Bs were inexpensive and chosen for that reason, with perhaps a secondary one being chatting with the homeowners instead of hearing just a grunt or two from an uninterested motel desk clerk.

But when they traveled to this country, B&Bs lost the inexpensive half of their appeal. While many B&Bs here are less costly than motel rooms, many others are just as expensive as commercial lodgings, and some are very pricey indeed.

But the folks who run them are usually far more affable than that desk clerk, and over here their appeal has flipped from the European cheap and friendly to friendly and perhaps cheap, but with distinctive decor and small touches that almost never turn up in motel or hotel rooms.

About Your House

Well, yes, you say, we've stayed at B&B's and know what they're all about, but how does the concept translate to our house? Surely, *our* humble, although quite adequate, abode can't become one of these places?

You say you live in a ranch home? A splitlevel? A bungalow? A farmhouse? A condo apartment in a high-rise building? A cottage?

Any of those housing styles can become successful bed-and-breakfast homes.

"You don't have to say, 'I can't have a B&B because I don't have a certain architectural style,'" says Jan Stankus, author of "How to Open and Operate a Bed & Breakfast Home" (Globe Pequot, 1995 3d ed., $14.95).

Adds Stankus: "It can work if there's a reason why people come to that area." That reason, she goes on to explain, can be a nearby college, where parents and visitors need a place to stay overnight.

Or you might live in a major tourist area, or even one with just one tourist attraction, such as a huge flea market or a wildlife preserve. Perhaps there is an active church or synagogue in your neighborhood, where many weddings are held, with nearby homes needed to put up guests. Or you are just a few blocks from a hospital or medical center where visitors, either to patients or to administrators on business calls, might need a place to stay overnight.

Maybe you are very near a corporate park or one or two large and busy corporations. Companies are increasingly looking to bed-and-breakfast accommodations for employees who visit them from other branches of the company, and for outside visitors. The B&Bs offer a nicer touch than putting those people up at a nearby motel and a safer environment, especially for women business travelers.

Faye Lynn and Hank Hollenbaugh got into the bed and breakfast business in 1994 because other folks just missed the boat.

The couple live on Anderson Island in Washington state. There is a ferry that makes the run from a spot near Olympia to their island, and then to another small island, Ketron. Faye Lynn Hollenbaugh works in a small store on the island. She found visitors to the store were often too late to catch the last ferry at night.

"I would offer to bring them back home with me until the next ferry in the morning," she recalls. "We didn't charge, of course.

"Then my husband and I started thinking about it," she continues. "Since we had in the back of our minds starting a B&B, we figured if we fixed up a room, we could then tell those people, 'We have a small bed-and-breakfast with a room for you.'" And get paid for their hospitality.

Thus Hideaway House was born, with one room for guests, not all of whom have missed the last ferry. Now the two plan to expand their operation. "When my husband retires from the military," Hollenbaugh says, "we plan to live on that pension and the income from the bed-and-breakfast."

So being near a ferry that runs only twice daily is *another* good reason for opening rooms in your home.

However, if you are in a traditional suburban community, with not much but houses and small shops around you, then you might have to pass on a B&B. Folks are not going to want to stay too far from the attraction that brought them to the area in the first place.

Stankus points out that location is at the top of the list for success here, as it is in almost every commercial venture.

Oh—and of course you will need an empty room.

You *can* offer just one room at your B&B. The average in this field is three bedrooms available to guests. A private bath for each room is certainly nice, but not necessary.

You say your home fits the above criteria? Next comes whether you *should* be welcoming B&B guests.

You and Your Family as Hosts

This is unlike other businesses in that these "customers" are not buying your product or service in a store, but are coming right into your home. Think about your reason for wanting to run this type of concern. It can't be simply money. For one thing, there isn't that much of it to be had, which will be discussed later.

"You can't go into this just for the money," Stankus explains. "I have met some of those people and they aren't that friendly and hospitable. This business is all about hospitality. People want to stay with you because they actually want to talk to someone who lives where you do. They want a little warmth that you don't get in a hotel.

"You have to be honest with yourself," Stankus says. "If you don't want people in your house, you will not be successful. If you are really a private person—and there's nothing wrong with that—you can't have privacy in a B&B, unless you work very hard to carve out some time and space for yourself.

"Some lifestyles are important, and take all our time, at different times of our lives. If you have three young kids, you may not be able to deal with a B&B operation, although I know some people who handle that very well.

"If you and everyone else in your family isn't for it, then don't do it," she warns. "I have seen splits in a family and you can tell who was for it and who wasn't. One host will treat you really warmly, and his or her spouse doesn't look at you."

A Closer Look at Your Place

There is still more to consider before opening your doors to guests.

Now you might give some thought to the interior of your place. Is your guest room (or rooms) attractive, or do you need to do some painting and decorating? Guests will expect a good mattress (the Hollenbaughs decided they should buy a new one for their B&B room) and soft pillows, and good lighting that includes a reading lamp. Plenty of blankets in the winter. A closet that does not smell of mothballs because your out-of-season clothes are hanging in the back. Some bureau drawers. Fluffy towels, not worn and thin ones. Most B&Bs have a television set in every room. If you choose not to, you will have to keep track of how often guests mention that lack, and might eventually have to buy one for each room.

Here is a more major concern than fluffy pillows: can you handle, say, six people, not to mention your own family, all taking showers in the morning? Maybe you will need another hot-water heater.

Breakfast, of course, is included in any B&B stay. You may learn you cannot serve a large, full breakfast due to regulations where you are. If you cannot, then be sure you serve something delectable—homemade muffins or cereal with fresh fruit or a special bread and jam. You cannot buy a Danish ring from the freezer section of your supermarket, pop it into the microwave and consider that breakfast. That isn't the done thing. (You can, however, run down to the bakery early in the morning for something delicious. It does not have to be homemade as long as it is tasty and special to your home.) Real coffee here, of course. And no powdered creamer. Place mats and perhaps a small vase of fresh flowers on the table complete a breakfast setting that is uniquely yours.

You are going to all this trouble because word of mouth is the greatest sales tool you will have. And every guest remembers the small touches—your sitting and chatting with them in the evening by the fire (you do not have to be available for conversation in the evening, but if you can and your guests want to talk, it's nice if you can do so), the afternoon tea you serve when the house is full so that guests can meet one another, or handing out brochures on attractions in town, particularly festivals being held on the days they are staying with you.

If, after reading the above paragraphs, you can see that converting part of your home to a B&B accommodation will be too expensive, then be wise enough to abandon the dream.

"Doing your math homework, you may find that it will cost you $10,000 to put your place in shape for guests," says Stankus. "You don't want to lose money here. The whole enterprise may just not be financially worth it."

Finally under this area comes the really fun part of the enterprise: give your home a name. No suggestions here. No doubt dozens of possibilities will occur to you.

Getting Started—Officially

Once you know that both you and your house can indeed be warm, friendly and accommodating to guests, continue to the next step. Look outside your home and seek local authorities' permission to run your B&B establishment.

First, look no further than the folks on your street.

Parking and noise are the two things you need to be concerned about here. If you have a driveway and just one or two B&B rooms, you're probably all set and nobody will care. If you are in the city and there is on-street parking with stickers for residents, you need to figure out the parking situation before your guests arrive.

"If your only option is for visitors to leave their cars in a no-parking zone, then red flags will go up," says Stankus. "You don't want to have your neighbors complaining about anything because they can shut you down."

Stankus suggests that you *not* go next to local officials, but rather make a quick detour first for some answers.

Each town's regulations are different, and even every neighborhood's. Some have strict fire codes, while others will make you change the plumbing in some way before you are licensed. If you are offering more than five rooms, you must comply with the Americans with Disabilities Act and make changes to your place that can be expensive.

If you go to the city without doing some research first, some officials might not know what they are dealing with, and so their immediate inclination is to say no. That reception is improving, though, as more B&Bs crop up, making the concept more easily understood. Actually, in many communities, because B&Bs are still fairly new, zoning laws can be murky about their legality.

Call other bed-and-breakfasts in your area and/or a B&B reservation services that serves your region. There are many of the latter around the country that serve an entire state or a portion of the country.

There is, for example, Bed 'n Breakfast Ltd. of Washington, D.C. (202-328-3510); Bed & Breakfast Down East, Ltd., serving Maine (207-565-3517) and Bed & Breakfast Hospitality Tennessee in Nashville (615-331-5244 or 800-458-2421), to name a few. For a listing of the statewide or regional service in your locale, write the National Network of Bed & Breakfast Agencies, Box 4616, Springfield, MA 01101.

Tell the folks you talk with what you are doing and ask whom you should talk to in local government.

Ask what problems they had setting up and what they would have done differently. Ask them what they charge for rooms, so you can judge how your accommodations differ from theirs and can set your rates accordingly. Then, armed with as much knowledge as possible about the way your community government is likely to view your enterprise, head for city hall to become licensed.

Another couple of points under getting organized: call your insurance agent to review your coverage as it relates to this new venture and talk to your accountant about the tax benefits or downsides of a home-based business.

Income

Let's see, you say. We have two rooms, and we've learned from asking around that we can get $65 a night. So that's $130 per night for Friday and Saturday nights only times 48 weeks (we'll take a month off), or $6,240 a year. That's a pretty good second income for just two nights a week.

It would be if you could count on it. But how many nights are you really going to be full during the year? Stankus says some hotels will tell you that a room occupancy of 100 nights out of 365 is considered pretty good, and hotels are usually in excellent locations.

"This is not a full-time living," Stankus adds. "That's one of the misconceptions I try to clear up immediately when I do workshops. You have overhead and you aren't going to be full every day." Not only is it not a full-time living, often it does not even bring in the money a second, or part-time, job would. This is something to consider. Many if not most B&B owners are in the business for the love of it, not the money. Just because you see thousands of B&B homes on the American landscape does not mean all those people set up shop because there is a killing to be made here.

Perhaps you will earn only a third of that $6,240, or a little over $2,000. Or maybe less. What will it take to cover your overhead? Your setting up expenses? Stankus hastens to point out you *can* make extra money once you get the hang of this operation. The questions are how much and whether that will be enough for you to consider the business a success.

Marketing

This is an important angle of your enterprise because no one can visit you if they do not know you exist.

"Some people get all set but never have a guest," Stankus says. "They never figure out how to get them. They're all dressed up, but there's no one there."

You can have a brochure printed about your place, give it to guests, and see if your local chamber of commerce or convention and visitors bureau will carry it in the racks of printed material they offer visitors to that area.

Here's another very workable idea: send your brochure to the head of the department of human resources (address that individual by name) at several large companies near your home, with a good cover letter, pointing out the attractions of your home and why their commuting employees and other visitors would be happier staying at your place than at a motel.

If your area already has B&B owners joined together as, say, Big River Bed-and-Breakfast, then you can join that group and can be marketed under their auspices.

Joining a reservation service is *the* way to go for most beginners. Here you will (for a fee, of course) gain maximum exposure, perhaps even in a book. The service will also help you set rates, assist you with marketing and in general do a lot of hand holding. "I even know reservation service managers who have gone to hosts' homes to help them greet their first guests because the hosts were nervous," says Stankus.

The Hollenbaughs do no advertising on their own, aside from a $3 advertisement in the monthly published on their island. But they do belong to a Washington state bed-and-breakfast reservation service, for which they pay a membership fee of $150 a year. With these kinds of services, members are generally written up in a brochure listing their homes, which is then sent out by the state's department of tourism to anyone making inquiries about vacations or other trips to that area. The reservation service also uses member listings when answering inquiries from would-be guests calling the service direct. Members who receive such referrals pay the services 20 to 30 percent of the total room bill.

Besides joining your own area reservation service, you might want to look into national books, such as "Bed and Breakfast, USA." You can be listed in that publication by joining the Tourist House Association of America (RR 1, Box 12A, Greentown, PA 18426; 717-676-3222).

A Marketing Twist

Obviously born marketers, Madelyn and Bill Berensmann opened A Cat in Your Lap, their bed-and-breakfast accommodation in Millbrook, in upstate New York. The hosts have assistance in helping guests enjoy themselves, in the shape, furry and round, of their two cats, Maxx and Moritz.

The fur faces are quite friendly, of course, and have the run of the 1840 farmhouse. However, they are not allowed in the two barn studios on the property that are also open to guests. Those who do not like, or are allergic to, cats can stay there.

The cats do not sleep in the guest rooms in the farmhouse.

"Occasionally a guest will let one in," says Madelyn Berensmann, "but then at 4 or 5 in the morning you have to get up and let him out, so having them in the room with you doesn't work too well."

The Berensmanns, who both hold full-time jobs elsewhere, do not belong to a reservation service, but rather market their B&B themselves. With the cat angle. Millbrook, while within easy driving distance from New York City for those who want a weekend away, has its own attractions, such as antique shops, wineries, horseback riding, and gourmet restaurants. It is also just a short ride to the mansions of Hyde Park and Rhinebeck. There are a number of actors who own weekend retreats in the community, so star-sighting can be considered another tourism draw.

Berensmann adds she also has a number of guests from area corporations, especially some international companies, "which I love," she says.

Without the cats, the Berensmanns' home might be just another B&B, albeit a striking and ideally located one. But when you have a very sociable Moritz answer the doorbell when you come to call, meowing loudly as the official greeter, you have one distinctive accommodation. And for the cat-lover visitor, a place that is extremely hospitable and homey. Just what a bed & breakfast should be.

SUMMING UP

$ Any style of house or apartment can become a successful bed-and-breakfast accommodation, given the right location.

$ The whole family has to want this enterprise. Indifference or annoyance will be readily apparent to guests.

$ Talk to other B&B owners or to your regional or statewide reservation service before getting local government approval.

$ Be sure you market your place well so guests can find you.

CHAPTER 13

Enjoy a Vacation on the House

By using it as a bartering tool.

This is an instance where your home *saves* you money, allowing you to travel about the world with no hotel charges, no stack of restaurant bills and usually no rental car fees.

You have no doubt read about home swapping over the last several years; a vacation style that continues to grow, especially in sluggish economies when the money for a vacation can be hard to find while the itch to get away remains strong. It is a simple concept: You stay in the Calvert-Smiths' home in rural England, while they are right here in your place. You feed their cats, they walk your dog. You trade cars too.

What's Involved Here

First, it should be said this is not a vacation style likely to appeal to those who are immediately saying, "Strangers in my house? Ugh." You need a certain spirit for these holidays. Those who think, "Hmmm, I've wondered about that," or "Tell me more" will probably go on to experience a very successful house swap, maybe choosing that style of traveling for many vacations to come.

It's not that you have to be willing to have perfect strangers make a mess of the place you call home. It's that you must be somewhat detached from "things" and more interested in experiences. Not that anything is likely to happen to your possessions if you vacation as a house trader. This is a concept that has been *very* successful in practice.

You can find swappers on your own by advertising in newspapers in areas you would like to visit, eliciting an exchange of letters and perhaps phone calls from those who respond.

The easier way is to join one of the nation's home swap clubs, which print directories of like-minded members, and those folks work out the exchange between themselves.

The directories have page after page of listings, of a few lines each, of members' houses or apartments. Your listing gives a member's address, number of people in the family, the location, what scenic or tourist attractions it is near, the number of bedrooms and baths, whether there are pets involved in the exchange, and where the member would like to vacation. Members interested in that listing write directly to the homeowner to make a match. Similarly, when you received your copy of the members' directory, you would pore over it until you found a house, or perhaps several homes in different areas, that appealed to you. Then *you'd* write. Many listings are accompanied by photos of the owners' homes, which range from quite nice to drop-dead lavish. Some come with *boats* a member can use!

"It's the only way to go," says Linda Lech, who made her first swap in 1992. "It frees up your money for other trips and special treats you would not otherwise be able to afford." Lech, who has a home along the New England shore, spent three weeks in a house in Belgium, touring Holland, Germany and Switzerland from her base there, and another two weeks based in France, tooling around that country.

Lech added the folks staying in her home had an equally enjoyable time touring that part of America and returned her home to her with no unpleasant surprises.

Next on her agenda, she says, is a visit to Italy with her mother and her two children. "We want to spend some time there tracing our family roots," she says.

Still a little dubious about the stranger-in-my home aspect of all of this? Remember, your swapping family is taking care of *your* home because you are in *their* place. You are each holding the other's house hostage, so to speak.

Karl Costabel, owner of the 16,000-member Vacation Exchange Club, the nation's oldest home swap organization, says, "If there's a common thread running though the membership in a home swap club, it's that everyone's easygoing." And, Costabel adds, very interested in travel, but often without the funds to see as much of the world as they would like if they had to spend vacation time and money on hotels. The Vacation Exchange Club initially was started by a teacher to give others of that profession a relatively inexpensive means of seeing the world.

"I find a lot of people get into this to save money," Costabel points out, "but they stay in because they enjoy the people they're meeting and the way they're living where they vacation"

That is another attraction of trading homes. By staying in someone else's place instead of the local version of the Holiday Inn, you are not just vacationing in, say, the south of France, you are living there—meeting your neighbors, shopping in local stores, finding your way around a European kitchen and discovering how local television differs from your own viewing options.

Even if you swap with someone in this country, there is the novelty of an entirely new (to you) section of America, with its daily paper, regional accents, specialty foods, etc.

Okay, you say, I'm sold. But I don't live in Florida or New York or San Francisco. Who would want to swap for my home in Upper Succotash?

You would be surprised. Every place in America has some features to offer a tourist, if not in that particular town, certainly within a few hours' drive.

There are swappers, too, who will want your place because it is in or near their old hometown. Or they want to visit grown children there. Or attend a class reunion or a wedding in or near your hamlet.

One important point about this—no, make that two. You must all, as a family, want to vacation in this style.

For example, while it might be great to have a kitchen where you can make your own coffee whenever you want it, a kitchen might mean more meals for the family cook than he or she would like when on holiday.

Also, swaps take time, usually about a year to wrap up. The home swap companies' directories usually are published once a year, with updates published throughout that year. Waiting for the directory, exchanging letters (and perhaps phone calls), means if you write today to one of the swap companies listed in this chapter, you probably should be planning a vacation 12 to 18 months from now.

Few Glitches

Those who run exchange clubs say there are very few serious problems with this vacation style and cite the fact that the clubs are still around—and going strong—after 30-plus years.

The principal problem—and it does not come up often—are swappers who change their minds after plans have been made, leaving that other family in the lurch come vacation time. Another concern can be difference in housekeeping standards, with some folks coming home to a house not as clean as it was when they left or disturbed in some other way. To avoid any unpleasant surprises, homeowners can spell out housekeeping expectations in the exchange of letters before the trade. That will include leaving instructions about trash disposal, recycling, mail delivery and the like.

Overall, these vacationers are sophisticated travelers, and are likely to heed your requests and special instructions. It is not unheard of, too, for vacationers to arrive at their swap home to find little notes all over the house giving instructions on how to run appliances and use certain gadgets and do's and don'ts for other areas and objects.

What about insurance? Since home swappers are essentially guests in your home, with no money changing hands, the typical homeowners or automobile insurance policy covers them. In effect, it is the same as if you had your in-laws over for a stay or were having a party in your home. You might check with your insurance companies to verify that you are indeed covered and ask for the same assurance from the family whose home you will be visiting.

Write Away

Here are some house swap organizations.

Vacation Exchange Club, PO Box 650, Key West, FL 33041, 800-638-3481 or 305-294-3720. The charge is $60 for three directories each year plus three updates.

Intervac International, PO Box 590504, San Francisco, CA 94159, 800-756-HOME, or fax 415-386-6853. One year's membership in this club is $62 plus postage, $55 for seniors. The directory carries more than 8,000 listings in 36 countries.

Intervac U.S. is an affiliate of Intervac International, serving as the American liaison for the parent company, and publishing a U.S.-only directory containing some 2,000 listings. There is one annual publication. A listing costs $35. Write Intervac U.S., PO Box 590504, San Francisco, CA 94159, 800-756-HOME.

Loan-a-Home, 2 Park Lane 6E, Mt. Vernon, NY 10552, 914-664-7640. Owner Muriel Gould says this club, with some 400 listings, specializes in long-term swaps or rentals. Clients are likely to be teachers, businesspeople and retirees who would like to live somewhere other than a hotel for a stay that will run longer than the typical vacation. Your listing in two directories and two supplements (one year of publications) costs $45.

If you would like to read more on this subject, try "Trading Places—the Wonderful World of Vacation Home Exchanging," (Rutledge Hill Press, 1991 [$9.95]). The authors, Bill and Mary Barbour, are Floridians who have made 40 vacation exchanges.

"The Vacation Home Exchange and Hospitality Guide" by John Kimbrough explains the exchange process and walks the reader through the steps leading to—and through—a swap. It comes from Kimco Communications, 4242 W. Dayton, Fresno, CA 93722. The price is $14.95 plus $2 for shipping.

SUMMING UP

$ Be sure the entire family is enthusiastic about this vacation choice.

$ Plan well ahead.

$ Be flexible in your geographic preferences. If you cannot make a match for the spot you want this year, try another locale. It's a big world!

$ Remember the principal problem with home swaps is the family that changes its mind at the last minute.

$ Spell out your housekeeping standards and ask your swap family what will be expected of you.

CHAPTER 14

Your Home in the Movies, or TV Commercials, Or . . .

"Oh sure," you say, "my house in the movies. Why didn't I think of that?"

Now, now.

This is, admittedly, a long shot. But read on. Maybe it's not such a stretch for *you*. Hundreds of movie location scouts and others all over the country are paying *very* good money to homeowners for the use of small parts of their houses. Think about the Hollywood movies and television drama specials you have seen recently. The characters were shown living *somewhere*, weren't they? And we're talking about others in the cast besides the stars.

Then there are television commercials, some filmed for a national audience and others shot locally to sell area products and services.

Beginning to see the possibilities?

Another fascinating part of this business is that lightning in the form of a handsome check for use of a part of their home strikes many homeowners more than once. Some homes are regularly used for filming.

What's Involved Here

There are a few points to keep in mind before you begin soliciting filming at your property.

One is that, as you have seen on the big or small screen, it is sometimes—maybe that should be most times—only a portion of a home that is used, rarely the entire dwelling. A dining room. A window seat. A den. So think of your home in sections, including the exterior of your property and even its view.

Also, for many uses you can forget your furnishings. Production crews usually bring in their own furniture and accessories to achieve the look they want, and move yours out. So no need to look around your place and say "Ugh, not with *this* living room."

You have a few avenues for getting the word out about your home.

Hollywood Films and Network Television Movies

This is very exciting, of course, especially when you throw in big stars coming to your place, all the paraphernalia around, the crowds watching behind the barriers. "Clear the set!" someone shouts. But maybe *you* can be close by because it is, after all, your house.

Start your path to film success with your camera.

You can immediately eliminate taking pictures of your house's upstairs. "Ninety-nine percent of the time we'll rule out any top floor," says Genna Goodwin, who with her husband, Greg, runs Goodwin Production Services, in Jacksonville, Florida. "We don't carry equipment upstairs. We need the ground floor and easy access."

Goodwin, who is also a location scout for films being shot in the area, adds that any rooms smaller than 12 feet by 12 feet will also be eliminated for consideration by her company. "It has to be large enough to accommodate a camera, some lights and a crew," she explains.

Take color pictures of your home—all of your home, except for the top levels—for a portfolio you will put together. Focus on the size of the rooms and their architectural details. "If you have high ceilings, be sure to get that in," suggests Pepper Lindsey, whose company, Lindsey Productions, Inc., is in Atlantic Beach, next to Jacksonville.

"They're good for working with lights." Note the height of the ceilings on the back of photos.

Be sure the pictures show that your home is an ivy-covered carriage house, or a farmhouse, or a loft, or yes, even a garden-variety splitlevel. They are used in filming too.

Take pictures of the outdoors as well. Do you have an especially attractive rock or flower garden? A circular driveway? A magnificent view of a lake, bay, river or ocean? A panoramic look at the city from your high-rise condo apartment? Click, click, click all over your place. Don't be stingy with size here. The photos should be at least 5x7.

You can write details about the rooms—dimensions, ceiling height, views, etc.—on the backs of the pictures. Lindsey suggests you also include the exposure from that room or outdoor view—facing west, a southern exposure, etc.

If your home has ever been written about—in a local newspaper's Home section, in a state or national decorating magazine—send a photocopy of that article, too. And you might include a map giving directions to your property.

Add to the pictures a cover letter asking that your portfolio be kept on file, why your home is interesting, and, if it is an old house, perhaps telling a little of its history. "I've had people get really creative here," Lindsey notes, "and send me a little story about the property."

You might want to buy one of those 8½-by-11-inch folders with the two pockets inside to send, so everything can be kept tidy and no photos are apt to get lost in the filmmakers' offices.

Send the package to the director of the film office in your state. Call to see who that is, and direct your package to him or her by name.

"There's a film office in every single state," says William Arnold, director of the North Carolina Film Office, located in the state capital, Raleigh. North Carolina has turned into quite a movie set over recent years, with such films as "Prince of Tides," "The Big Chill," "Conrack," "The Great Santini" and others filmed there.

"We do keep what residents send us on file," Arnold continues, "and I expect the other offices do too."

Mail it, and then forget it. Don't call them, they'll call you. There is no way they can use your home unless a need arises for just what you have to offer. So don't follow up on what you have sent unless things change and you have added something new to your home (or have moved). If you have made some additions or upgrades, then send a whole new kit. Your cover letter might then say that the package enclosed replaces and updates the one you sent on such and such a date.

It does not happen often, but occasionally opportunity will come a-knockin' without your having to lift a finger.

A Near-Brush with Fame

Carol Carlino, who lived in a brownstone in a small community in the New York metropolitan area before moving to another part of the country, had three members of the production staff for the network series "Dream Street" visit her home in the late 1980s. You never heard of it? Read on.

"They called first and asked if they could come over and look at the house for the show," Carlino recalls. "I said sure. So three of them walked from room to room and said almost nothing to one another. Then they said 'Thank you' to me and started to walk out. I didn't want to bother them with questions, because frankly I couldn't imagine their using my house, so as they left I just said, 'So, you're considering this one too, huh?' And one of the men said, 'Yes, we're looking at a few places here.' He handed me his business card, and that was that.

"I honestly can't remember now if they ever got in touch with me to tell me my house wasn't chosen, although they probably did. I know we had a lot of location shooting in my town, and we were all talking about this particular show. I ultimately did find out which house was chosen, although I'll never know why that one was and mine wasn't. The show ran just a couple of weeks before it was canceled. Low ratings, I think."

Carlino played it correctly, not asking about money or anything else at that preliminary stage. If the group had been chattier, she might have said, "So, what exactly are you looking for?" but that's about the most you can contribute to a house search. The structure, its layout, architectural style, grounds or whatever will have to speak for themselves. You cannot do a sales job here.

The Local Scene

Here is how national work filters down to where you live. What is likely to happen at the state level is that filming companies contacting state offices are given the names of local production companies in the cities or towns where they want to shoot their movie. In large cities that have their own film offices, a producer might head straight for that film chief. The out-of-towners, no matter how they reach the local level, eventually work with local production companies and scouts.

Pepper Lindsey, for example, spent part of the summer of 1994 as associate producer working with a crew making two ABC made-for-television two-hour movies.

You want to get your portfolio to production people in your own town, too. Jacksonville is typical of how cities have viewed filming in recent years—as a money-maker and great public relations for that community. A metropolitan area of one million residents in the northeastern part of Florida, Jacksonville has its own film office as part of city government and a sizable number of production companies that film national and local television commercials and corporate, nonprofit and training videos. For the most part they work with local advertising agencies and corporations, sometimes hooking up, as Lindsey did, with national producers who have come to town to film movies or television programs or commercials to be shown nationwide rather than locally.

You can get the names of production companies in your area from your state's film office. Send them your portfolio. If you live in one of the large cities that has its own film office, hey, send a kit there too.

A few very large cities—New York, to take one example—also have individuals who have formed companies exclusively to scout locations. If you live in one of these locales, send the scouts your portfolio as well.

All in all, local productions are likely to provide you with the most opportunity.

Genna Goodwin, for example, has shot commercials for a leading regional furniture store, for a regional bank, for the local advertising of a national hardware store chain, and other area companies.

It is local advertisers who are the bread and butter of these producers.

Your Competition

It can be difficult breaking in here, just as it is with any area that is new to you, because while your house may offer a gorgeously decorated and architecturally splendid patio, so might someone else's in town. Sometimes it's who you know who wins the job.

Charlie Barth and his White Hawk Pictures, Inc. operate out of Jacksonville, too.

"Often what happens," he explains, "is that somebody knows somebody who knows somebody who knows somebody who has exactly what you want, whether you're looking for a nursery with windows all around, or an old-fashioned kitchen, or a brand-new one."

That is understandable, since once the word goes out within a production office for what is needed, there is bound to be somebody who knows somebody, etc.

That's how Lynn Oves, who lives in Atlanta, came to have her baby carriage used in the film *Pet Sematary*, from the novel by Stephen King. Oves had not used the carriage in five or six years, but was storing it in case family or friends needed it in the future.

"It is a rather ordinary carriage," she says, "of cloth and a little metal—we aren't talking expensive English perambulator here." The company paid her $100 for two weeks' use of it.

"A cousin of mine was set designer for the movie, which was filmed in Atlanta," Oves explains. "She came into town and went around to a lot of different shops that had items she needed, and set up a leasing program with them. She asked me if I had this or that item, and when she came to the carriage she said, 'I'll rent it from you for $50 a week.'"

Busy local production companies often use the same house again and again, too. It saves time looking for new properties, it has already been proven to work and it's familiar.

Shannon Graham's Jacksonville home has, she says, been on film nine or ten times over the last two and a half years. "It's nothing fancy, by any stretch of the imagination," Graham explains, describing her home. "It's a two-story, stucco, traditional house of about 3,600 square feet. But it flows well for their needs, I think. We have some open spaces."

That is a major key to success—open areas versus partitioned rooms, that will accommodate equipment and staff people.

How did Graham come by her good fortune? You guessed it.

Genna Goodwin knew Graham through a mutual friend, and when Goodwin was shooting at Graham's sister's house (her sister's had her home filmed too), Goodwin told Graham exactly what she was looking for next. In short order, Goodwin and her crew were at the Grahams' home, shooting the family room.

Graham and her family enjoy the comings and goings, but Graham herself takes a rather laid-back approach to seeing her home in area commercials. "I'm always surprised when they call me," she says. "I've never looked at this as a money-maker. If it's convenient for us and for them, we just do it."

Back to You

Don't let the foregoing "knowing somebody" deter you from sending your portfolio and industriously pursuing work for your home. You do not know what a producer is going to need next, and indeed neither does he or she.

Can you bargain over what you are being offered for use of your house? Well, the money offered is usually quite generous. Genna Goodwin says rates in Jacksonville start at about $200 a day, "but when I go to New York to rent," she adds, "I've paid $1,000." So there it is again, that magic location, location, location that sets different price tags on homes in different locales, even their daily rental rates.

Rates can also be all over the place, depending on how deep the pockets are of the movie or television producer or product sponsor or whoever is authorizing the shoot. To some degree rates depend, too, on how much of a house they will use and how many changes they have to make. If they are going to repaint a room and then paint it back again, you will get more for your trouble than if they are simply going in and filming

"Simply" in the above sentence is probably the wrong choice of word here. There is nothing simple about filming, especially on location. "I tell people we'll be bringing in a small army," says Pepper Lindsey, "and that we'll have cables all over the floor. But you should see the look on their faces when we all pull up. They just don't believe it."

Yup, you can have 35 or 50 or however many people it takes to get things right, all of them walking in and out (your floors will be protected), trucks parked out front (producers usually get permission from the city), doors left open, noise and an overall busyness. "I just ask them not to smoke in the house," Shannon Graham says, "and if they're outside not to throw the cigarette butts in the yard."

The producers or production companies carry insurance for this extravaganza, so no need to worry there.

Your contract with the company also will state that the crews will leave the house as they found it.

Naturally, you will lock up valuables while the horde is working and make sure your pets are out of the way.

You may be asked to leave during filming, or, if the shoot is taking place in one small corner of your house, you might be allowed to stay.

You can look in and watch as your home makes its way to stardom!

SUMMING UP

$ Having a part of your home or property chosen for a feature film or network television movie is a long shot, but worth your covering all bases by sending a portfolio to those who make these decisions.

$ Take the time to make that portfolio as attractive—and comprehensive—as possible. It's your only contact and sales tool.

$ Don't bother anyone after you have sent the kit. They'll be in touch with you if and when the need arises.

$ You will be offered a contract spelling out your agreement with the producer or company. If you want any special clauses added, speak up and ask for them.

CHAPTER 15

Growing Fruit, Veggies and Culinary Herbs

How is your garden growing these days? The one that feeds you, not the merely pretty one.

If you have no outdoor space, you're excused for flipping through these pages to the next chapter. If you have xeriscaped your yard to within an inch of its low-maintenance life, you too might want to pass on this.

But if your yard hasn't been touched in more time than you would like to admit, you are letting slip by an opportunity to make and save money. That patch of green or brown, no matter how small, can provide food for the family table. Your own, and others' too.

What's Involved Here

One of the favorite topics of all of us is the increasing price of food. "Do you know what they charged me for one tomato?" "Can you believe this teeny bottle of basil cost $1.68?" "You spend money for a head of lettuce, and by the time you've trimmed it down to the good leaves, you've thrown away half of it."

Don't want to take it anymore?

Fight back. Grow some of your own food.

Turning part of your yard into a garden providing you with some of the foods you eat daily will of course save you some money, but it will also become a fascinating hobby that's good exercise. It will offer you some virtually no-cost gifts for family and friends. And for the truly ambitious, it can bring in a little cash when you sell what you grow.

Oh, and the food is likely to taste better than what you buy at the store, according to small-time gardeners.

Dana and Klem Adamski read about square-foot gardening and decided to give it a try at their central Florida home.

"We wanted something that was manageable," Dana Adamski recalls, "gardening we could do in the evening or on weekends, since we both work. We have a pool in our yard, too, and don't have a whole lot of available space. And also, when it's real hot in the summer, you don't want to be out there working. All of that led us to square-foot gardening, and we've had a lot of fun with it."

Two years after its start, Dana Adamski is still enthusiastic about the couple's garden patch, tossing out gardening terms and offering advice for the newcomer to the world of the vegetable garden.

Here is how their raised bed garden is set up, a commonly used approach that could certainly work for you too

The Adamskis built frames from 2-inch-by-12-inch treated lumber. They made three beds 4 feet long on all sides for traditional garden vegetables, and one bed 3 feet wide and 4 feet long for herbs.

The two chose raised beds because the Florida soil is sandy. Raised beds are also a good choice for the novice, since they give the gardener control. You buy the *exact* ingredients for a soil as nearly perfect as you can get for what you want to grow and do not have to work with what your yard offers or is lacking.

The Adamskis filled each bed with a homemade potting mix, consisting of topsoil, cow manure, vermiculite, peat moss and a sprinkling of lime.

Each of the 4-foot-square beds is divided into 16 equal segments using nails and string for delineating, and then the transplants or seeds are added.

The number of vegetables per square depends on the eventual size of the plant. For example, you might grow only one tomato plant to a square (yes, tomatoes are fruit, but are almost always used in the context of vegetable), but a similar-sized spot could hold four lettuce plants or 16 carrots.

Concerned about neighborhood birds and squirrels getting into the beds, the couple also made lids for the boxes. They are about 5 feet 5 inches high, of chicken wire and bamboo sticks around a wood frame.

Their bible for all of this was *Square Foot Gardening* by Mel Bartholomew (Rodale Press, $14.95).

The couple have now also "harvested" corn, snow peas, spinach, lettuce and chard. They've sown beans at the back of the garden where the vines can climb a chain-link fence. "When you don't have that much of a harvest," Adamski notes, "you get really particular, and you want the odds for growing in your favor."

In all, Dana Adamski estimated the couple's investment at around $125.

Their garden produces enough food for the family, with some to share with relatives.

Some small gifts, too. When they had a run on parsley, Adamski says she gathered a bunch, wrapped it in attractive paper, like a bouquet, tied it with a ribbon and gave it to one of her neighbors. "I've given lavender cuttings to people, too," she adds.

Coming up next for The Little Farm in the Semi-Tropics: refining the corn they've started growing. "We've already had our first crop," Adamski says, "which we did on a lark. We didn't believe it would grow, but it did. We had 14 stalks, with a few ears on each of them." For the corn, the couple had to remove the lids from the beds, of course. One crop that will be continued on and on is buttercrunch lettuce. "There's nothing like it," Adamski enthuses. "It's a small lettuce, but it has a completely different taste when you pull it out of that garden."

About Fruit

You don't have to live in Hawaii to grow luscious fruit in your backyard. "Apples will grow way up north," says Linda Naeve of the Iowa State University Horticultural Garden in Ames. "Pears will grow in Minnesota." While conceding that there are limits on where, say, peaches will come in nicely, Naeve says you might be surprised at what will grow in your neck of the woods.

If your local or state university has a horticulture department, by all means call and seek its guidance. Many public gardens around the country also offer advice on growing habits of fruit, herbs and vegetables (not to mention flowers, trees and shrubs).

Getting Started

Interested? Ready to begin digging? Confused and overwhelmed? Have a dozen questions? All of the above?

Naturally, these few pages can offer just an infinitesimal bit of information for the novice produce gardener.

- To expand your knowledge and guide you through the planting, tending and reaping processes, you can buy and gobble up gardening magazines. There seems to be a growing number of them at the newsstands these days.
- You can also very easily have a book direct you, the way the Adamskis did with "Square Foot Gardening." The Gardening section of your bookstore is likely to be so refined these days that you can buy a book not only for what you want to grow, but for your geographic location, how much space you can allot to a garden and how much time you want to spend in the yard too. Someone has written a book for just about every narrowly focused audience.
- Your all-time best bet for help with a new garden, however— and this office has been mentioned before in this book—is your county extension service, which is listed under County Government in your telephone book, perhaps under the Department of Agriculture in your county. Almost every county in the nation has one of these services.

  Help from the extension service is free. You can visit the office in person or you can call. You can write for the booklets it offers. You can attend any special lectures or workshops it sponsors. All for free.

  You might already be familiar with this agency from your local paper. Many agents, as the staff people are called, also write columns for a newspaper's weekend Home or Real Estate section, on a variety of gardening subjects and problems.

Dana Adamski took a route you may want to consider. Two years ago, when she had taken a year off from work, she signed up for the master gardening course offered by her extension service. It was a comprehensive program, one day a week for eight or nine weeks, covering all aspects of gardening. The course was free. In return, Adamski was required to spend 50 hours a year working for the extension service on a volunteer basis. For the most part, she has staffed the hot line phones that ring constantly with homeowner questions, but she has also worked with 4-H students in her area. "There are a lot of ways you can put the time back," she says.

Fifty hours a year for how long, you ask? Weeeeelll. As long as you can offer the time. The exact term isn't carved in stone. You are not required to take this course and put in community service if you only want to ask occasional questions of the extension service staff. Adamski wanted to learn all the master gardening program had to offer.

The master gardener you will meet in the next few paragraphs—a designation you are given after completing the program—has logged some 2,500 hours of volunteer work.

Phil Braunschweig is a master gardener for the extension service in Seminole County, Florida, where the Adamskis till the soil. Like Dana Adamski, Braunschweig volunteers his time to answer homeowner queries.

The extension service does have a paid staff. There is an urban horticulturalist, for instance, and a few others skilled in specific areas such as 4-H programs, home economics and the like. But because of budget constraints in most county offices around the country, it would be impossible to help the members of the public with their many questions without volunteers.

Many volunteers are especially knowledgeable in one area under the huge extension service umbrella. Braunschweig, for example, considers indoor plants his specialty. Besides answering innumerable telephone calls from home gardeners, he also talks with county residents who stop by the extension service office for advice. Usually, he says, they bring with them a leaf or a dead vegetable or a chunk of a tree bark.

"I've had three people in here already this morning," he says, at 9:40 *AM* one Monday.

Do consult these folks when you need a hand with your green thumb. Someone there is sure to be able to analyze your problem and come up with a solution. You can call or visit more than once, too. There are some home gardeners Braunschweig calls "regulars," that he and others assist frequently.

Back to your home garden. What are some good crops for the beginner? Dana Adamski picked some almost surefire successes with hers, adding that the novice might also consider tomatoes and peppers, which, she says, are not difficult. She also notes beginners might want to start with seedlings rather than seeds.

Linda Naeve adds you almost can't go wrong with green beans, cabbage, peas, lettuce and other leafy veggies.

The Herb Garden

If growing fruit or vegetables is not quite your cup of tea with lemon verbena, then why not try a herb garden?

Most herbs are not that difficult to grow and, as you know, a pinch of this or that enhances the flavor of many otherwise quite ordinary dishes.

You can have a windowsill herb garden, the window usually being in the kitchen, with a southern or western exposure. Or you can plant your garden outdoors.

Madalene Hill, a nationally known herb gardener and author of several books on the subject, has her own thoughts on a windowsill lineup. "It's all right if you're continually under six feet of snow," she says, "and you have a sunny window. But most houses are probably too dry and don't have the circulation of air to make herbs grow as well as they will outdoors or in a greenhouse."

Hill, who is based in Texas and is the author of what might be called the "perennial" on the subject, *Southern Herb Growing* (by Madalene Hill and Gwen Barclay with Jean Hardy, Shearer Publishing Co., 406 Post Oak Rd., Fredericksburg, TX 78624, $29.95 plus $5 for shipping and handling) adds that two other common errors keep many neophyte gardeners from success in herb growing. "Drainage is essential," she explains. Everything else is secondary." She also points out, "They don't grow in those little containers. People wonder why their herbs aren't growing and yet they haven't replanted them, either in a larger pot or in the ground."

Finally from Hill, "Trim the plants often. The more you cut them, the more they grow."

You might want to start your herb garden with fairly easy plantings almost guaranteed for success: the perennial herbs, such as parsley, thyme, oregano and sage.

Selling What You Grow

While on the subject of herbs, the ones you grow at home should delight your family and perk up many dishes, but are not likely to be saleable to others. Says Linda Naeve: "You'd need a lot of volume and a controlled environment, such as a greenhouse, to sell herbs. Otherwise they will probably be too small and a little spindly."

If you do want to get into marketing herbs on a serious level, you can contact the International Herb Growers and Marketers Association (IHGMA). Composed of 600 members who are beginning growers, longtime gardeners, retailers, educators, writers and those interested in the medicinal uses of herbs, the IHGMA offers printed material, tapes, conferences, trade shows and more to members. Annual membership is $80, and Kathy Sebastian, a spokeswoman for IHGMA notes, "You don't have to be a member to partake of what we offer, but obviously it will all cost less for members. This is a caring, sharing group—I don't know what new members will find more beneficial, the networking or the educational aspect."

Want to sell your vegetables and fruit? A roadside stand might be successful where you are.

Biz Fogie, who with her husband Tom runs a farm that is open to guests (more about her in Chapter 19), had a stand for several years, selling the produce from that spread.

Fogie says the three most important tips she can offer roadstand sellers are: location, location, location.

Naturally, if you live on a heavily traveled road you are going to be more successful at this than the backyard farmer on a cul-de-sac. Indeed, folks in the latter situation will not even consider setting up shop where they are.

Fogie no longer runs her stand, as you will see in Chapter 19, but she offers some other pointers to those who would like to turn their harvests into money.

- Check with your municipal or county office to see if you need a permit for a stand. Fogie did not where she lives because her stand was considered part of her working farm. If you do not have a farm, you might need permission.
- Be sure your stand is out of direct sunlight, which can burn up the produce. Have a little roof over it, too, for protection from rain.
- Make it as attractive as you can, with lots of fruit and/or vegetables on display. It should look full and plentiful, Fogie says, not skimpy.
- Make signs so that those driving by will know, without having to get out of the car, what you are selling and the prices you are charging.

- Price a little lower than the supermarket at first. "I went up a little year by year," the Pennsylvania farmer points out. "Remember, what you're selling is organic, grown in good soil without the need for pesticides or other chemicals. Eventually, I was pricing higher than supermarkets, but I still couldn't fill the demand."
- Make sure you are always open at the same time each day or over the weekend, so people are used to your being there. Staffing the stand? Fogie didn't, figuring her time spent on the farm growing still more produce was more valuable than manning a roadside stand. She left a cashbox with a sign requesting buyers to take the produce they wanted, and leave the money for it in the box. If they needed help, they were asked to blow their horn, or come up to the house.

    That honor system worked in Fogie's quiet part of Pennsylvania. It might not where you are, and you may want to have a family member at your stand at all times. Fogie concedes she did empty the cash box periodically, so as not to tempt buyers. "I took in the Abe Lincolns and left the Washingtons," she says.
- Don't be concerned about the competition. There will always— if you live in a rural or semirural area—be folks doing what you are, but Fogie says there seems to be room for all. A neighbor down the road from her, for example, sells tomatoes, just tomatoes. But Fogie also sold them, and found buyers picked up some of hers when they were buying other items from her stand, so her tomatoes sold too.

Here's another money-making opportunity: If your yard is large enough for a fruit patch of some size, invite the public in to "pick your own." Let them fill boxes of blueberries or strawberries or whatever you are growing. One woman who had an acre of blueberries on her land earned between $25 and $100 a day in season! You'll have a bigger profit if you ask buyers to bring their own containers. Run a classified advertisement in your local paper giving details.

Finally, there is the farmer's market. Call your state's department of agriculture to see where markets are in your area (you probably are already familiar with the one closest to you). Usually you will have to pay a small rental fee for joining a farmer's market and will have to follow their rules for selling. For the most part, that means you sell only what you have grown yourself. There might also be some health laws regarding the placement of your display (not on the floor, for example).

You know from your own trips to a farmer's market that the little table with the fewest products does not do nearly as well as the table bursting with produce, with items for sale piled up on tables, stacked against poles and hanging from overhead hooks. If you want to sell a smaller lot of products, you might add to your stall some of your homemade jelly or cakes, or perhaps handcrafts. Homemade is the ticket here, of course.

Naturally, you will have to abide by the market's restrictions on exactly what can be sold. Some farmer's markets have a wide latitude and some stalls could, aside from a few items of produce, almost be situated in a flea market. Others hold strictly to selling only what comes from the soil.

You might also make some calls on local produce merchants in your town. Bring along a sample of what you are growing and tell them how much of that product you can guarantee them if they are interested. Another suggestion: If you are growing peppers, *lots* of peppers, ask around at pizza parlors and perhaps busy, casual-style Italian restaurants. They use peppers by the ton, figuratively speaking, and often buy and freeze sizable supplies at a time.

The Community Garden

If you live in an urban area with few or no backyards for planting, here's a thought. If there is a small vacant lot near you that is owned by the city, get in touch with your council member and ask if the residents of your block or neighborhood can run the patch as a community garden. You might be allowed to till the soil there free or at a nominal rent, for an indeterminate amount of time or until a buyer is found for that plot of land.

If the lot is privately held, you might ask the owner if you can have a garden until the parcel is sold.

Each of you in the garden group will have a square of land on which to grow whatever you choose. These cooperatives foster a sense of community spirit and pride, can lead to a lifelong hobby for those taking part and can produce some delectable food (which will probably taste even better to you knowing it came from seeds or seedlings you planted).

SUMMING UP

$ Look to the pros for advice on a new garden, especially the no-cost county extension service where you live.

$ Start small. You can broaden your repertoire as you gain confidence and as your small garden produces healthy fruit and veggies.

$ If you want to sell what you grow, you will have to think like a marketer and produce crops in volume, suitable for sale to the public.

$ Look to the community garden for a cooperative experience that will produce more than merely food.

CHAPTER 16

Don't Hold A Garage Sale Before Reading This!

Some consider them money-makers. Others say they are visual clutter on the landscape of America's neighborhoods. They are garage sales, or yard sales, or block sales. In high-rise apartments they are lobby sales, and in row-house enclaves they are stoop sales. They are a dab of entrepreneurialism any homeowner can profit from, and most of us have tried one at some time or other.

Some are homeowners who hold garage sales to get rid of stuff before they move. Their primary interest is seeing buyers haul away unwanted goods so there is nothing, or virtually nothing, left to take to the next address. The money received for those items is a secondary concern.

Then there are the money-minded, who envision pots of cash at the mention of the words "garage sale." These are the folks who milk events like this for all they are worth—and walk away with a very nice pile of change.

If you are reading this book you are likely to be in the second category.

Thinking about having your first sale? Then you should know there is more to making money than setting up the folding aluminum table on the first nice weekend in the spring, covering it with jelly jars, mismatched dishes and other bits of this and that you no longer want, plunking down a "garage sale" sign in front of it all and waiting for live ones.

The pros know that the secret to making money in this crowded arena is preparation. Here is how to get ready.

What's Involved Here

- You might have to get a permit for your sale. Some municipalities call for them, while others have no requirements on the books. Because of what they see as abuses—people holding a continuous garage sale *for several months running*—many towns will allow only one, or two, or four sales per year per household. Check with city hall to see how these enterprises are viewed in your locale.
- Check your homeowners insurance policy. You will no doubt find that your coverage will protect you from accidents that might happen to customers during your sale. However, if you hold many of them during the year, that may term you a professional in the eyes of an insurer. If you have any doubts about coverage, call your agent.
- Next, decide when to hold your garage sale ("garage" will be used throughout this chapter, although you may well be having a sale somewhere else on your property, or even at a flea market table several towns away).

    A very important consideration: Schedule it so that you have time to plan adequately. Asking the family, "Hey, guys, what say we have a garage sale Saturday?" is not likely to bring you the profit you will realize if you allow two or more weeks between the idea and the sale.

    When scheduling, avoid weekends when there is likely to be a conflict with residents in your town participating in major local events. Eliminate holiday weekends for the most part, too, although if you live in a tourist area those days can be a prime time for sales.

    Weather should be reasonably mild and clear. Is a rain date necessary? Probably. Or at least keep one in mind. Browsers might not come out in even a slight drizzle.

- Should you hold a sale Friday, Saturday *and* Sunday? Or just Saturday and Sunday? Or just Saturday? That will depend on how much you have to unload. If you think you can keep tables filled through the weekend, go with three days. You might ask family and friends if they would like to contribute to what you have, or have left, to give the sale a fresh, crowded look each day. (Naturally, they will take payment for their items, unless they have told you to keep it, which they might well do if they are more eager to be rid of the stuff than paid for it.)

- Try to get another homeowner on your block to hold a sale at the same time. In fact, the more the merrier—and more profitable. Folks like getting out of the car just once and being able to hit several tables. If you do not know your neighbors, print or write a flyer to go under doors that tells a little about your plans and asks for others to join you. Give your phone number for response. Another advantage of a few households joining you: you can split the cost, although it is a minor one, of advertising the sale in your local paper and buying material for signs.

- Organize your inventory. Since you are Really Serious About Making Money, look around at every item in your home and consider whether you really need it and like it. No? Out it goes. If you are not using it right now place it in the "garage sale" pile in the garage (or basement or walk-in closet). Keep a list of furnishings and other items now in use that you will come back for on sale day.

A caution to retirees here: don't become so enthusiastic about paring down that you sell too much. When Joyce and Bob Fitzpatrick moved from Wisconsin to their Florida retirement home, they held a successful sale, but one that Joyce Fitzpatrick now looks back on with regret. "Furniture prices are so high," she says, "and we ended up having to buy some things we sold back home for practically nothing—expensive furniture we had acquired over the years that is priced astronomically now if you have to buy it new." Fitzpatrick adds it costs far less to haul anything you think you could possibly need to your new home than it does to buy it new. You can always hold a garage sale at your new address if you have brought too much furniture with you.

On the subject of moving south, many retirees and others heading for Sun Belt areas feel they should rid themselves of heavy wood furniture they are certain will be out of place in a geographic area strewn with wicker and light colored furnishings. Not true. Many bring cherry and mahogany with them, and intersperse those woods with light colors and fabrics. It is called "colonial furnishing," named after the English decorating style for homes in colonial India.

You do not need big-ticket items to hold a successful garage sale. Most first-timers are amazed at what sells.

"We had three egg cups," recalls Carolyn Janik of her first garage sale. "I priced them at $1 each, and they were among the first things sold. They were 20-year-old cups, and the fourth one had been broken years ago, so they weren't even in a set!"

Janik and her family were moving from their home in the New York metropolitan area to Connecticut, selling as much as possible that they had acquired over the 20 years of living in that 10-room house. Their sale ran Saturday and Sunday and they realized, Janik says, "almost $500." The most expensive item that sold: an exercise bench priced at $50. Second most costly? A pool table that brought $25. "We didn't have any big items at all," she says.

The family across the street from the Janiks held a sale the same weekend and made almost as much.

- Look for the gold before digging out the tin. You probably do not have a Van Gogh in your attic, but it is possible there are other valuables tucked away there—or in the closet or in bureau drawers or basement cartons. We all hear stories of garage sale and flea market shoppers who come home with silver buried under decades of grime, rare coins, paintings no one else knew the value of and so forth. You might think you have nothing but junk stored, but a closer look could happily prove you wrong.

  Any item that is questionable should be taken to a jeweler or antique shop owner or other specialist for an appraisal. For example, many of us have inherited boxes of miscellany from our parents or other older relatives, items that were of no particular value then, and at first glance seem useless to us now. Well, maybe they *are* worth something, and wouldn't *that* save you having to hold more garage sales!

- Advertise your sale. You will have to let folks know there is a sale going on in your place, especially if you are somewhat off the beaten track—out in the country, perhaps, or in a quiet cul-de-sac with no through traffic. Signs at major intersections can help, especially if you follow them with more signs leading directly to your home (your municipality may have rules about signage, which you can ask about when you are looking into a permit). Some radio stations announce local garage sales. And most newspapers have special rates for garage sale ads, which usually run Thursday, Friday and Saturday. Put up notices on supermarket bulletin boards and at other places that attract attention and passersby. It will cost a little to publicize your sale but, as the saying goes, you have to spend a little to make a little, so do not keep a lock on your wallet if it means the difference between a good sale and one with one or two browsers who found you because they were lost.

- Get the kids involved. You will need help on sale day, and they can be kept busy bagging purchases, explaining how gizmos work to customers, making change and keeping an eye on the tables to be sure no one walks off with items. The kids can be paid a percentage of the day's take or a flat per-hour fee. Or maybe they will simply keep what they sell of their own, after cleaning it up and pricing it.

  Here's another idea: If your kids are very young, they might want to bake cookies or brownies and sell them with lemonade at your sale. Another money-making avenue for them.

- Price to sell. You do not want to see the same tired merchandise still on the tables at the end of the day, do you? But how much to ask for it all can be a puzzle, especially for the first timer. Probably three different homeowners would look at, say, a blender and set three different prices. Some say 10 to 35 percent of purchase price is about as much as the market will bear for old but not valuable items. Price a little higher than what you will ultimately take for the item, so you can be flexible when customers want to bargain. They will expect to, and you will be expected to give a little. Part of the fun of a garage sale for shoppers is not only getting something at low price, but also bargaining down the seller to an even cheaper figure.

  You can use tags or stickers on what you are selling, but whatever your choice make sure every item has a price on it somewhere. Pricing, as you can see, is a very important part of this event and it can be nerve-wracking to have to come up with prices during the course of the sale.

- Looks count, so wash, polish or otherwise spruce up what's for sale to make those items more appealing. One woman puts an "It works!" sticker on hair dryers, mixers, lamps and the like, although some customers wanted to check those items anyway. She has an outdoor electrical outlet that can immediately answer their question. Have a mirror so shoppers can try on jewelry and scarves.

- Have plenty of change and small bills on hand. It is a given that the first several buyers will hand you $20 bills for 50-cent items. Also start saving brown bags, plastic supermarket bags, and newspapers for wrapping china and dishes.
- Be ready early—very early. Sales draw the greatest crowds from 8 AM to around noon, but early birds will hover around your home from about 7 AM. They are likely to be dealers who resell your goods at large flea markets, antique shop owners or collectors looking for the truly valuable and frequent garage sale shoppers, who know the good stuff goes quickly. Be prepared to be interrupted even while setting up for the sale. Hey, be prepared to have the doorbell ring while you are still stumbling around in your bathrobe sipping coffee!
- Keep security in mind. You will need at least two workers at your sale, so that someone is always watching the cashbox— and the shoppers. Theft is common at these sales. One woman joined a neighbor's large sale in the neighbor's driveway. She had only a small card table, with a few appliances on it and on the floor beneath her feet. A dozen items tops. Not much to keep an eye on? Someone walked off with one of her coffeemakers, and she had no idea how it happened. Keep the door to your house locked, too. If someone wants to use the bathroom, ask one of your "staff" to escort him or her inside, or direct the shopper to the nearest public facilities.

    If you have your cash box set up at the end of the tables, as folks leave your driveway, you (and your assistants) can see who is walking away with what. Never leave that money box unattended, of course.
- Change sale strategies as needed during the day. As mentioned earlier, mornings will be times of peak activity for your sale. As crowds taper off in the early afternoon, you might want to slash prices and have a sign that says "everything 30 percent off" or something similar. You can put small stuff into grab bags for $1 or $2 apiece. Unsold books can be "two for the price of one." Make your table look enticing to the drive-by shopper, even when the pickings are rather slim.
- Give some items away. The Janiks had a ton of kids' games. "We just put; a big sign on them marked 'Free,'" says Carolyn Janik. "And we had 'free games' in our classified ad." Freebies

always attract buyers, and since, in the Janiks' case, games were not the focal point of their sale, giving them away was a good idea. Some sellers also give, rather than sell, religious items.

Magazines are slow movers, and Reader's Digest Condensed Books are not even lifted up and paged through. You might give them away. (Your public library will probably not want the Reader's Digest books either, even for their fundraising book sales.)

- Consider a variation on the garage sale—the indoor or outdoor flea market. For a fee of $10 or $15 you can take a table at one of these extravaganzas and do very well for yourself.

Jeannie and Al Bowden have had three garage sales at their various Virginia homes, but it wasn't until Jeannie's cousin Michelle told the two about a flea market that they became hooked on the large-scale sales.

"It was winter, and we were going to move," Al said of their first venture, "and Michelle had been going to an all-year-round indoor flea market held every Saturday in a fraternity organization's hall. There must have been room for 100 tables, plus ones set outside if the weather was good. We booked a table because we just couldn't hold a yard sale in February, and we sold almost everything. I couldn't believe the number of people, and they seemed willing to buy anything."

The Bowdens paid $10 for their table and made $365 that day. They moved within easy driving distance of the flea market hall, and have been back twice since then (stuff does accumulate, doesn't it?).

You might see these sales advertised in your local paper. Frequently, especially in bad weather, tables are reserved in advance and the good spots can be signed up quickly. The regulars, too, eat up prime space, so newcomers are often relegated to off-spots. Al Bowden said they were in a sort of annex to the main hall, but there were still hordes of people, making no spot really undesirable.

Wrapping Up

Richer, and certainly tired by now, you will probably fold up shop around 3 or 4 PM, unless there is a lot of activity where you are and still much to be sold. You can put remaining merchandise in boxes and take them to the nearest charity pick-up (do not forget a receipt for income tax purposes), or you can haul it all back into your garage for the next sale.

You ought to drive around the neighborhood and take down those garage sale signs, too.

And congratulations! By following prescribed preparation steps, you have almost certainly realized the greatest possible profit. Hard work? Maybe. But how long would you have had to work at your day job for that same amount of money? Keeps it all in perspective, doesn't it?

Finally, if you'd like more to read and you are holding a sale because of an upcoming move, ask your mover's agent for any booklets that office might have on conducting garage sales. Many large national moving companies do publish a good deal of printed material that is offered to customers at no cost.

You also can write for "Holding Garage Sales for Fun and Profit," by Bob Berko, available for $6 (which includes postage) from Consumer Education Research Center, PO Box 336, So. Orange, NJ 07079. The 108-page booklet is chock-full of tips, including an interesting chapter on accepting goods on consignment.

SUMMING UP

$ Plan a sale well in advance, to allow you suitable preparation time.

$ Try to get support from neighbors, so you can hold a block sale.

$ Price everything carefully, remembering that everyone will want to dicker over what you are charging.

$ Advertise! You can't sell what nobody sees.

$ Don't sell anything that might be truly valuable—at least not for $3 at a garage sale.

$ Have plenty of change on hand.

$ Be ready early. More than one homeowner is made an offer at 7 AM for the whole batch of stuff.

CHAPTER 17

Teaching a Class at Your Place

Piano? Voice? Auto maintenance and repair? Cooking? Dog obedience? Baking? Writing? Quilting?

What is your particular skill? Teaching a handful of students how to do what you do best is quite possible for almost anyone at home. While it is not likely to bring in *big* bucks, it can be a relatively easy way of earning a small steady income. It can also be a nice little ego boost when you see how much you know in one specialty, how good you are at imparting your knowledge and how very receptive your audience is to what you have to say.

What's Involved Here

First, you should know that to teach these types of courses, you do not need an impressive academic background. All that matters is that you know the subject you want to teach well. Very well. You cannot have your students knowing more than you, so if need be you will want to bone up on your area of expertise before advertising your services.

Next, a direction you have read often throughout this book—you ought to make sure you *can* teach at home. This is frequently a grey area, however. While many zoning laws restrict businesses operating from residential areas, teaching an occasional class, where you would not alter the exterior of your dwelling, jam the street with parked cars or hang out a shingle, is often permissible.

Ruth Charnes informally held cooking classes in her home in a small, older city in the East. That crowded metropolitan area has a mix of commercial, residential and retail buildings with, it seems, no discernable zoning pattern. Also, street parking—there are no garages with these houses—is impossible for everyone, so there could be no neighbors to complain that Charnes's students were taking up *their* parking spots. In any event, the students walked to Charnes's home.

Charnes taught cooking to eight to 11 grade school students attending a private academy less than half a mile from her home. The principal approached Charnes, whom she had known for several years as a noted cook in the community. She offered Charnes $15 an hour for each 1½-hour class, plus payment for supplies used. The classes ran only through the academic school year.

Charnes taught for several years before joining her husband on his frequent business trips often kept her out of town during the school year, causing her to relinquish the class. She loved the teaching experience, she says, and laughs often while talking about her experiences with measuring cups, flour and sixth graders.

Having been there, Charnes offers several observations that should be helpful to those considering that minicareer. Teaching cooking was certainly a busy time for the cook, she found—before, during and after each class. Planning the day's "meals" to be cooked (starting with simple food, such as omelettes and salads, and working up to making the student self-sufficient in the kitchen) took time. Shopping for groceries to be used in each class was even more time-consuming, and the class itself kept the teacher hopping.

"I was exhausted on those days," Charnes recalls, "between demonstrating, and watching them cook, and keeping track of the time to make sure dishes weren't overcooked, and then trying to get everyone to clean up. Actually, *my* cleanup time took as much as an hour."

Another point, and an important one for the would-be cooking instructor, Charnes notes: "There was a good deal of wear and tear on the kitchen. In fact, that was the reason a friend of mine stopped teaching cooking."

Charnes also cautions about the safety factor of teaching her class. "Since you're dealing with cooking," she says, "you have to keep a careful eye on your class, especially when it's children." The academy provided insurance coverage for the class, which she found reassuring.

Cooking requires supplies, of course, and scurrying around in the kitchen.

Brian Curtin taught writing around his dining table, a far calmer "school" setting. Curtin, who is self-employed with a writing/consulting business, taught nonfiction writing at a local junior college's no-credit adult education program Saturday mornings for two hours.

The writer, who lives in Illinois, was paid $30 per hour for the six-week course at the college, or $360. The students paid $75 apiece. Curtin needed seven students for the course to be held each semester, and he did have that many enrollees for the fall and winter semesters of the first year he taught. Then he signed up to teach the summer session, but just three students showed up.

"I sort of shrugged to myself," he recalls, "and told them that the course would be held again in September, and I hoped to see them there. I also mentioned there might be other writing courses held during the summer in the area, and they might check around if they didn't want to wait until fall.

"After I made my announcement, and was getting ready to leave the classroom, the three women came up to me and practically pleaded with me to teach the course outside of school. One even offered her office for a classroom. I took their names and said I'd think about it and get back to them."

Curtin thought. He lived in a community of single-family houses with garages, and he felt there would be no problem with the women's cars parking in his driveway where they would not interfere with street parking or traffic.

He decided he would teach them for three weeks, two hours per week, at $75 apiece, or $12.50 per hour per student. He felt the market would not bear a fee any higher than $75, and he did not want to teach the college's 12 hours because with only three students his hourly fee would have to drop too low.

The course was, he felt, very successful. He enjoyed the teaching, and the students told him they appreciated personal attention. Some three months after the course, one of his students called Curtin and very excitedly told him she had sold her first magazine article. "I think I was as excited as she was," he recalls.

Curtin returned to teaching at school for the fall term, and then again in the winter. Both classes had more than the seven students required. But after the second semester that year he opted to retire from academe.

"I got busy with my work," he explains, "and just thought the course took too much time for the money preparation time, that is. I suppose I could have started an all-day writer's seminar in my area, charging a pretty good amount of money, but I decided to drop the whole teaching thing."

Two stories, two very different ways of falling into teaching at home. As you have seen, neither of the aforementioned teachers conducted classes long enough to collect gold watches. Adults who are busy in many areas of their lives often find that when something's gotta give, it's the class they teach. Sometimes, too, after a few classes, teachers find the market for their specialty has been tapped. This is especially true in small towns and cities. Eventually, everyone who is interested has taken "The Weekend Woodworker" course. But while it lasts, it can be great—and teachers of these specialized courses always learn something new during a class, whether from a textbook or a student.

Here are some pointers if you are already thinking how you would handle instructing in *your* specialty:

- Be sure there is a need for what you want to teach. For instance, if there are several craft shops in your area offering courses, your teaching quilting or other handiwork might be an overabundance of available instruction.
- You may want to specialize. There might be no takers for a course with the ho-hum title of "Cooking." But watch students line up to sign up for "Chinese Cooking," or "Healthy Heart Cooking" or "Baking for Chocoholics." Or perhaps "Down Home Country Cooking," since there are bound to be more than a few folks who'd like to know how to make meat loaf that isn't dry and mashed potatoes that aren't lumpy.
- If you are teaching auto maintenance and repair, you will probably hold your class in your driveway. That will certainly be a giveaway to neighbors that you are running a business, no matter how small. If you live in a community bound by homeown-

ers' association bylaws, working on any car other than your own for profit might be barred. (Yes, to put a fine point on it, you will be working on your own car, but it *will* be for profit).

- Walk the slender line between earning as much as you can from your course and setting a fee too high to attract students. Carefully gauge your time per hour based on what you think it is worth, considering your skill and the need for training in that specialty.

  Take into account, too, supplies you will need, and whether you or your students will buy them. If students need to buy a particular textbook, be sure to tell them that cost will be in addition to the course fee.
- Publicize your classes (and remember, if you have not done your zoning homework, publicizing in your neighborhood will give away your plan) with notices on area bulletin boards, in newsletters of houses of worship and perhaps in weekly local newspapers.
- Prepare some sort of lesson plan. You don't have to stick to it— it's *your* course, and sometimes discussion veers away from the topic into areas even more interesting—but you should have some general idea what you will cover for each of the three or six of however many course days you will be teaching.
- Some home teachers take only cash or money orders for tuition payments, while others will accept personal checks. It's up to you.
- Keep in mind summer can be pretty dead for course-taking. Winter might be slow, too, since January brings postholiday bills and many residents of your community will no doubt be unable to afford the nonessentials for a while. September is a time of renewal for schoolchild and adult alike, and is the best time for an elective course. Naturally, that is broadly speaking. If you are teaching swimming at your home pool, or a holiday crafts session or two in October, you will be right on the mark.
- A bit of a drag: you probably will have to clean house (or at least a portion of it) for your class, which can be a nuisance if you are pretty busy with a day job, small children, etc. But you are a teacher, not a grand host or hostess here, so there is no need to put out the paté and take drink orders. Curtin and his wife did a minimal amount of cleaning up before a class. He served coffee or tea, and told students they could bring their own bagel or

Danish or whatever (the class ran from 9 to 11 AM). Sort of a brown-bag breakfast.
- Finally, be energetic and enthusiastic. You want to impart your love of the subject you teach to those who are eager to learn. Give it your all.

If you are excited about teaching a skill you love and know well, but cannot see how you can conduct a class from your condominium apartment, or your house with four small children underfoot, or for any other reason, do not let your dream slip away. You can contact colleges in your area to see if you can teach noncredit courses at their adult education school. Or call your local school board, which conducts adult education classes in the evening at area public grammar and high schools.

Or you can look into teaching a course at a business or organization related to your specialty: handcrafts at a store that sells crafts materials, for instance, or swimming at the local Y, or watercolor painting at an artists' supply store.

Approaching a nonprofit organization may result in a teaching assignment—but with no fee for you and little or no charge to students. If you want to undertake this volunteer work for personal enrichment or for credits to add to a resume, go for it. You are talking about a field you love and will no doubt have an audience eager to learn. The money can come later as you become familiar with the instruction process and decide where you want to take the teaching talent you now have and the subject matter you know so well.

Good luck, Mr. (or Ms.) Chips!

SUMMING UP

$ Consider zoning regulations where you are.

$ Be sure there is an interest in your community in what you want to teach and that the market is not overcrowded with instructors in that specialty.

$ Prepare at least a rudimentary syllabus for what you will be covering during the class.

$ Be enthusiastic and energetic about your subject.

$ If you cannot teach at home, look to outside business and community organizations for an opportunity to talk about your specialty—and bring home extra cash.

CHAPTER 18

Opening Your Home to the Public—Occasionally

"Why, my dear, your home is so lovely you should charge admission."

Every hear that about your place? Seriously.

There are any number of private residences around the country that are distinguished historically or architecturally, furnished handsomely, and with owners who would be only too happy to show guests through—for a price, of course.

Receiving compliments is a nice little ego boost for the homeowners, and let's not forget the equally nice little piece of change charged for touring the house or using it for a special event.

In this chapter you will meet two homeowners with quite different and distinctive properties who are earning a second income from opening their doors to an appreciative public.

What's Involved Here

First, exactly what kind of houses are we talking about for this kind of money-making endeavor? Well, we'll have to eliminate ranch or splitlevel homes and most types of new construction.

The house that visitors will pay money to tour might be the one downtown that dates to the early nineteenth century. Or that huge farmhouse down the road, near the site of the Battle of Whatever. Or the row house in a city neighborhood that is, along with its neighbors on that block or in that conclave, on the National Register of Historic Places.

For the most part, think old. Think historically interesting. Think an architectural gem from another time. Think at least a few rooms, certainly the parlor, or downstairs, carefully furnished with a few antiques, perhaps wallpaper or other furnishings or accessories in keeping with the period.

Think houses that could have appeared in the pages of *Colonial Homes*, *Traditional Home* or *Victorian Homes* magazines.

Doing a flip here, you might also think new, but only if the house is startlingly different architecturally, large and decorated superbly. The sort of house that you have driven by and thought, "I wonder what that looks like inside. I'd be willing to pay $3 or $4 to see." *That* kind of home.

If any of the above sounds like your place, you can make money by opening your house only occasionally, at times that are convenient to you.

Janet Sourk is a single mother with four young children who lives in the Schuster Mansion, a three-story Italianate single-family house in the Hall Street Historic District of St. Joseph, Missouri. The style of the house is, as you might imagine, very ornate. Built in 1881, it sits on two acres of land and is smack in the center of the district, which is on the National Register of Historic Places.

Fortunately for Sourk, the house was never, as the saying among preservationists goes, "remuddled" over the years. Virtually all the splendid architectural details remain.

"It's really lovely," says Sourk, "probably one of the better homes in St. Joe. It remained a single-family home and has never been turned into apartments."

Sourk had her eye on the house for several years before buying it in 1991. "I've just been in love with this house since I first came to St. Joe in 1981," says Sourk, who is originally from Kansas. "It took about 10 years for me to get it, though."

When she bought the property, Sourk applied to municipal authorities for permission to have the house converted to a bed-and-breakfast accommodation. While she still offers two bedrooms to guests, she is now just as involved with tours and special events at the mansion.

At this point it should be mentioned that Sourk has a full-time job away from the house. However, she explains that activities at the Schuster Mansion, while now taking several hours a week, could, if she had the time (and, no doubt the energy), become a full-time career. The potential is there.

She got her start when friends called to say they had a friend who wanted to hold a wedding and/or a wedding reception at the mansion. Was that possible? Sourk replied yes, certainly. "I'm licensed by the city to be a tour home and to offer special events," she said.

Today Sourk allows tours of the formal front part of the first floor, the upstairs hall and two bedrooms on the second floor. "We keep five closed off because I promised my children we wouldn't have people walking through their bedrooms and gawking," Sourk explained.

She adds there are other tour homes in St. Joseph, "and those people don't have four young children." Those other folks might open more rooms to the public. It is up to the individual homeowner to decide what spaces can be viewed by a touring public, although they must, of course, show enough rooms to make a visitor feel the tour was worth the price of admission.

Thanksgiving and Christmas see many tourists walking through the Schuster Mansion, Sourk says. "We decorate big-time for Christmas," she points out, "and do Christmas parties."

Weddings, wedding receptions and private parties are all booked at the mansion, but Sourk notes she does no cooking. All the meals are catered—"I'm not licensed as a restaurant," she says, adding, "I can accommodate 150 to 175 for a reception, and up to 80 for a sit-down dinner. It depends on the function." She uses four rooms in the formal area of the house—there is no one large room.

Fees

Sourk charges $4 a person for a tour. The group rate is $3 per person, those visitors usually coming in from a bus tour. Tours are by appointment only, and Sourk is listed with the St. Joseph Chamber of Commerce, a source of much of her tour activity. She also advertises in the Yellow Pages of her telephone directory under "Wedding Services" and "Reception Halls." She notes most of her calls for weddings come from the Yellow Pages.

Her fee for space for a wedding or reception is $550. That does not include food, beverages or table setups.

Sourk advises anyone considering this kind of sometime open house should think carefully about rates. "It's a lot of work, but what you have is unique and gorgeous. Don't price yourself too low. I called around to all of the rental halls in my area, and then listened to friends who said I have something special and I should set a price in keeping with what I have to offer. And that's more than a $100-a-night hall."

Sourk adds that when you consider how much time it takes to clean and set up for an event, the price is reasonable. Not to mention the time spent with the partygiver. She notes, "I have brides come over and sit down and talk at least an hour on the first visit, and after that I spend more time with them on the phone. Then there's the day itself and the day after, when people come back and pick up extra chairs and things like that. So there's a lot of time spent before and after the event too."

Next for the Schuster Mansion, Sourk says, is upgraded landscaping. "I'd like to have gardens to tour," she explains. "We have several mansions here with incredible gardens. There are a lot of possibilities here that I'm looking forward to getting into."

Over in the Keystone State

Sally Hassinger is a full-time teacher. Ken Hassinger is a full-time auctioneer and farmer.

Both open sections of their home on a part-time basis for banquets and private parties.

Situated on 175 acres in Pennsylvania Dutch Country ("but we're not in the commercialized area," Sally Hassinger points out), the Hassingers have quite a sizable complex, which includes a turn-of-the-century farmhouse with four bed-and-breakfast rooms rented to the public and an addition to the house that was Ken Hassinger's grandfather's barn. The barn was moved to the house site and reworked into living quarters for the family and an enormous 32-foot-by-32-foot room that is open to the public.

There is another large building on the site called the Apple Storage because that's what it was years ago. That space is also available to rent. There is also a log house and eight log cabins that can be rented.

A small art gallery is on the grounds, and all around is a working farm with ducks, chickens, turkeys, horses, black sheep and more. It is all called Mountain Dale Farm, and a busy place it is.

While the grounds are available for outdoor parties and the like, it is the 32-foot-by-32-foot room and the Apple Storage that see the most activity when it comes to renting space occasionally. "We have banquets for the Kiwanis," notes Sally Hassinger, "and we have the Sierra Club here three times a year for meetings. We provide meals and a business setting in the Apple Storage and they pitch tents on the farm grounds."

The 32-foot-by-32-foot room, which can seat 45 comfortably for a banquet, is decorated with antiques and interesting wall art. But the "art" outside the structure might be the most eye-catching of all. "All you see from the huge windows are fields and trees," Hassinger says.

The Hassingers, who started their farm on a small scale in the late 1970s and have seen it grow a little each year since, advertise their facilities. For several years they circulated a pen and ink promotion piece they put together themselves. Now they have a brand-new, full-color brochure. Their spread has been featured in magazine articles, which is terrific free advertising and exposure.

Hassinger feels there is a sizable market to be tapped of business-people, artists and others who want to hold meetings, parties and the like in unique settings. She charges $95 for a room rental if guests want to bring their own party decorations and refreshments. Since she does offer meals, she charges $15 per head for a full-course banquet for a minimum of 20 persons.

The downside to all of this? "No privacy," Hassinger says quickly. But she and her husband have two small children, too, and she concedes it is rarely quiet around Mountain Dale Farm. "My phone rings constantly," she says. "You hang it up and it rings again." In addition to their accommodations and party facilities, Ken Hassinger's business is home based. That means more phone calls.

Since both Hassingers hold full-time jobs, what do the other money-making activities at the farm constitute? A part-time job? A hobby? "This is what you would call a major hobby," Sally Hassinger says, adding that expenses—animals, crops, buildings, taxes, etc.—connected with running what sometimes seems like a village almost eat up profits. "It's a labor of love, though," she adds. "Absolutely

Your Home on a Tour Circuit

Does all of this sound like something you could do, too, given your home and a block of time you can spare to conduct tours, keep your place sparkling clean and organized, and do a little promotion of what you have to offer? Here are some suggestions for getting started.

- Approach your local government to see if you need a license for opening your house occasionally as a tour attraction.
- Look into regulations for serving food if you want to get into that aspect of an open house.
- Visit open houses in your state to get a sense of what goes into those productions.
- If you are interested in private parties only at your home, and no touring visitors, you will have to market your enterprise. That will call for a brochure, perhaps a listing in the Yellow Pages and in your city magazine, if there is one. Learn to highlight what *you* have to offer that most commercial places do not—namely history, a homey atmosphere, unique and beautiful furnishings, etc.
- Are you in a historic district? Or are there other old homes near yours or elsewhere in your community? You might do well to band together, call yourselves something like the Historic Homes of New City, and then try to interest your area chamber of commerce in listing your group and plugging it in the reams of printed material it offers the public. Perhaps if you create a brochure featuring all your homes, the chamber will agree to use it in promotions or have it available in its office so tourists can become acquainted with your area.

  This can work for just one home if you find no takers on a group idea, but then your home will have to be spectacular.
- Whether there is one homeowner or several in the area interested in this idea, you can also contact your local historical society to see if it would be interested in helping you set up tours. Staffers there can be extremely helpful, of course, in helping with the historical background of your house.
- Before approaching either of these groups, decide just how often you want to open your home (every Wednesday from 10 AM to 3 PM, for example). Indeed, put together your presentation, covering all areas of what you want to accomplish here, so you

are confident and able to answer any questions. You will focus on why the public will be interested in visiting your home and why that tour will give your town more to boast about and more for visitors to see.

- To get your tour project or private party facility off the ground, you might want to (or have to) do a tour at no cost for a non-profit group. Or charge no rent to a group that will have its brunch or dinner catered. That way word will spread about what you have to offer in your old or historic home. You will be out the hundred dollars or so you would otherwise have charged, but you will have reaped valuable exposure, and even more priceless word-of-mouth references that are likely to follow.

- In doing paperwork for this project, check your homeowners insurance policy and talk to your agent about any changes that might be needed in your coverage.

SUMMING UP

$ If you have a beautiful or historic or architecturally significant home, you can open it to the public only sometimes, at dates and times *you* choose.

$ Look for support from your chamber of commerce, a local historical society or any other group that would have an interest in seeing your old or historic home publicized. That's not financial support, but rather an endorsement of sorts, and some help in spreading the word about your project.

$ Do all the behind-the-scenes work before going public with your open house. That includes licensing and insurance check-ups.

CHAPTER 19

The Farmer Takes
a House Guest
or Two

Have you been clucking lately about ever-rising expenses around your farm?

Here is an idea that will bring you extra money and a totally new way to view your farm operation.

Biz Fogie might serve as your inspiration.

Eight years or so ago, Fogie and her husband Tom had a 21-acre farm in Lancaster County, Pennsylvania, an area of the Keystone State that is primarily agricultural. Their spread was small—a few animals and a sizable garden where she grew strawberries and asparagus.

"We were hippie-type farmers," Fogie recalls. "I also had a health food store in a small building attached to the farmhouse. It was sort of an extension of a roadstand I had out front."

Fogie, like any businessperson, wished for more customers and then opportunity knocked, totally changing the family's farm operation.

"I saw an item in a Lancaster farming newspaper," she recalls, "that said you can have guests coming from the city who will pay to stay at your farm. We thought about that, and decided to convert the store into a little apartment. We called it 'The Chicken Coop' and began taking in tourists."

The couple also added a pair of peacocks as a little extra visual stimulation for the city folk. "We let the animals run loose," Fogie notes.

As they had time and money, "we worked our way up," as Fogie explains, painting and redecorating two bedrooms in the farmhouse that are now also open to paying guests.

Today the—what else?—Olde Fogie Farm is open to visitors year round and is one of the most popular farm vacation spots in the county.

What's Involved Here

There is probably not as much work whipping your place into shape as you might think. City folks, especially those with small children, want to visit a working farm, no matter what the farmer's specialty, because it is interesting and different. You don't need to change anything.

They are comfortable with the homey atmosphere and prefer to dress casually. They're on vacation!

Also, motel stays can be nerve-wracking for adults with rambunctious kids in tow. Letting the little dears run around farm acreage, or be quietly occupied fishing or watching and taking part in farm chores, can be relaxing for parents and huge fun for the small set. Their "land" back home might be a front lawn, if that.

There are a *few* formulas for success here, however.

The Farm Itself

"Working" farm is the key, no matter how small your spread and no matter what your specialty. There is much for vacationers to see and learn about staying at a tree farm, an orange grove, a dairy. . . or at your place.

What you will be offering tourists is a personal look at farming—not just by spending a few nights at a farmhouse but by tooling around with the farmer on his or her rounds, listening to talk about the business and, perhaps most intriguing of all for the city slicker, pitching in and helping a bit. If you take your guests with you as you collect eggs, for example, let *them* do that chore, a small thing for you but something for them to talk about back home, and for quite some time, too.

Getting Permission

As you might expect, you must get permission for your proposal from the local governing body. What you are offering is a variation of the bed-and-breakfast concept but there is enough of a difference between the two to warrant a separate chapter for each in this book.

If bed-and-breakfast inns are allowed in your community (or, speaking more broadly since you are in a rural area, in your county), then you probably have only to follow the steps regulating those accommodations to set yourself up as a farm host. You might be limited to offering just two or three rooms, which should be fine with you since you are not, after all, interested in becoming a full-time innkeeper.

Another angle working in your favor when you trek down to city hall or the equivalent: farms, by definition, are on a fair bit of land, so your immediate neighbors are not likely to complain about traffic congestion around your place or your guests' cars hogging on-street parking spaces.

The Buddy Factor

You can undertake this sideline alone, just you and your family. But what might work better is seeing if there are other farm families in your region or throughout the state who can join you. (If there are and they are already organized into a farm host program, then they can help you with starting-up information.)

Let's go back to Pennsylvania. Farmers offering vacation accommodations there had been in existence since the 1940s, under the aegis of the state Department of Agriculture. The program existed to educate residents and others about the rural environment. When a budget crunch hit those offices a few years ago, the program was picked up by the Pennsylvania Travel Council, another state office.

"Agriculture is our number-one industry," says the council's Debbie Bowman. "Tourism is our second most important industry."

Bowman adds she and her office publicize the 19 farms that are now part of the program in the state.

It should be noted here that farm vacations are popular in Pennsylvania because there is a huge population to support the program by vacationing in the area. Visitors come from New York City, about three hours away, from Philadelphia to the south and from the dozens of New York City bedroom communities in north New Jersey, offering a vacation pool of several million persons. That's not counting the millions of Americans outside that tristate area and Canadians, many of whom also want to visit Pennsylvania farm country.

If you are in a state that is predominately rural, you have a different situation and a much smaller tourist pool. Even folks in the metropolitan areas of your state may have grown up on farms or still have relatives farming. There is not that novelty that can be marketed, although there will likely always be a small pool of interested tourists.

But if you have a farm within a few hours' drive of a population center where there are certain to be city folks who have never even seen a country lane, you just might have a hot ticket.

The Host and Hostess

Taking in paying guests will make an enormous change in the group dynamic around your place. Biz Fogie says it is the farm wife whose life will be altered the most. She will almost certainly have to abandon some or most of her farm chores to care for guests. She will at the least have to be *around*, a visual presence of the family as hosts, while the rest of the clan and any day workers are out there making the farm run.

Both host and hostess will also have to really *want* to see their paying company, and not consider them a mere business sideline or, worse, a nuisance.

The kids will have to be all for this adaptation, too. Fogie's are now grown. Her daughter was in her twenties when the farm was changed to accommodate guests, her son around 13 when the real business began. Says Fogie: "Kids, especially teens, can be rude and embarrassing around guests if they don't like this idea. My son was never like that, but he was a little shy sometimes. What he did was give up his room to sleep on top of the barn, just him and the dog. They'd troop up there every night.

"We did over his room for guests and called it the Pig Pen. He made $2 for every night guests stayed in that room. He's had a raise since those days and now gets $4 a night."

Sharing in the profits or earning a flat fee can do a lot to turn a kid who simply does not want to mingle with guests into a farm vacation booster. Of course, children should not be pushed into any activity surrounding this business if they are just not interested. Guests will pick up their lack of enthusiasm, not to mention their outright annoyance.

What Else Should You Offer?

Most farmers offer a sizable breakfast for guests, which is sometimes included in the room fee. Guests take lunch and dinner away from the farmhouse. Breakfast is probably what you have right now, perhaps your weekend fare. Simple and hearty and right at your kitchen or dining table.

You will be expected to know what and where the tourist attractions are within a few hours' drive of your farm. Guests will likely leave the house just after breakfast for sightseeing. The more brochures you have around, the happier your company will be. It wouldn't hurt you to investigate tourist draws yourself before opening your farm doors, so you can say with authority exactly what Antiques Row is and whether picnics are allowed in the state park.

In the evening your company is likely to be tired from touring. Sitting on the porch, rocking and chatting will be fine with them, while the kids run around the place. They might like to spend a few minutes talking with you, so if you can spare the time, that is a part of their vacation—and your service—they will remember. As you become more familiar with the host concept, you might plan a small event in the evening, especially if you have a house full of guests. Fogie, for instance, occasionally has campfire sing-alongs, and for 50 cents apiece takes guests on a half-hour hayride. She does not babysit guests children. "No way," she says emphatically.

How Much to Charge

Thought you'd never get to it, you say. Well, there is a reason for talking money this late in the chapter. You can no doubt tell by now whether visiting your farm would be a novel experience for people in your area of the country and whether you would be a talented host. You might be willing to put a higher price tag on a stay there now then you would have earlier in the chapter.

What you charge will depend on what the market will bear and whether you have much farm competition or strictly B&Bs as rivals. You will have to take into account how much you really have to entertain visitors; the time of the year—high season, off-season or somewhere in between; whether the guests' rooms have a private bath and even whether the rooms are on the first, second or third floor. You might have different rates for different rooms.

Biz Fogie charges $50 per night for the efficiency apartment, which has a fully equipped kitchen. Those guests do not have breakfast at the house. The rooms in the house rent for $60 a night for a couple, $10 for each child. Those rates include breakfast.

You can decide whether you want to accept guests all year round, or just at certain times. Most farm families welcome a breather from guests in the off-season, but the phone does not ring that much then anyway.

Publicizing Your Vacation Spot

Publicity is important here, as it is in most businesses. If you are opening your farm by yourself, you will need to advertise in newspapers and magazines read by the market you are seeking to attract.

Most likely, however, there will be a few of you who have banded together and called yourselves something like Piccolo County Farm Vacations. Then you have several marketing approaches.

Debbie Bowman suggests first asking your state's department of agriculture to assist you, which will not only take some or all publicity chores off your hands but will also lend weight and credibility to your venture. You can also, she adds, contact your state tourism office for assistance.

"Agriculture is on the decline in many parts of the country," Bowman explains, "so farmers willing to share their homes with visitors and show them how a farm runs are likely to be greeted with enthusiasm."

Sponsorship is not likely to be free, however. Biz Fogie and the 18 other farmers listed in the annual Pennsylvania Farm Vacation Guide the Pennsylvania Travel Council publishes pay $1,000 annually for the states spreading the word about their farms. That money goes for an annual black-and-white brochure about the farms in the group, which is sent around the country and to Canada in tourist packages and taken along to travel shows the staff attends. Here is how the Olde Fogie Farm was listed in the 1994 brochure:

Name, address and telephone number, and then . . .

We love sharing our Lancaster County life with our guests. Been farming without chemicals for over 20 years. We are an "Old MacDonald–type farm" . . . have everything but a llama . . . and thinking about a llama, too. We spend time each evening with our guests doing the chores, milking the goats, feeding baby goats with a bottle, gathering eggs, feeding pot-belly pigs, etc. A great place to rest and regenerate. Enjoy the gazebo by the pond in the evening, or have a picnic there. Horseback riding available. We receive guests year-round. Tour nearby Hershey, Lancaster Amish areas, historic York, Gettysburg and historic Marietta.

Accommodations: Two different plans: live with us in our old-fashioned home with its Amish-type stove and Biz will provide breakfast, or guests prepare breakfast in a private, quaint, efficiency apartment within our home with its own entrance.

The Fogies also spend $100 a year for publicity garnered from membership in the Pennsylvania Dutch Convention and Visitors Bureau, which publishes the brochure "Farm Vacations at Lancaster County Bed and Breakfasts," listing 26 working farms that provide lodging in Pennsylvania Dutch Country. That brochure is not given the exposure of the one from the travel council.

She adds she spends no other money on publicity, brochures, advertising and the like, although some farm hosts in the state do conduct additional publicity campaigns on their own.

You might also find sponsorship for your group through the regional or national association for your specialty. Have a dairy farm? Maybe there is a state trade association that would be interested in advancing the idea of farm vacations. The brochure that lists the Fogie farm has an interesting line in the text that reads, "This publication was printed courtesy of Pennsylvania Rural Electric Association." See how many groups in various sectors might be interested in your venture?

Finally, look to colleges or universities in your state. In Pennsylvania, Penn State's College of Agriculture has produced the states Bed & Breakfast Business Plan Workbook for owners of those establishments and has worked to publish other material to inform and guide farmers and other homeowners in this hospitality specialty.

Sold?

If you are about ready to add one more money-making facet to your working farm, both the sources quoted in this chapter offer assistance.

Bowman's office will send material on bed-and-breakfast accommodations and farm vacations in that state, which includes rules, regulations and start-up information for owners. All of that can be useful by analogy where you are. Write Pennsylvania Travel Council, 902 N. Second St., Harrisburg, PA 17102.

Biz Fogie is happy to talk to any farmer around the country interested in starting a farm vacation accommodation. She asks only that you restrict phone calls to between 10 AM and 9 PM EST time. She can be reached at 717-426-3992.

SUMMING UP

$ The whole family should be enthusiastic about this undertaking.

$ Your place can be small, as long as there are genuine farm chores to show interested guests.

$ Start small—one room, when it is ready for guests, is fine.

$ If forming a new group of farm hosts, look for sponsorship or any other kind of support from a trade association, corporation or school likely to be interested in promoting farms or farm products in your area.

PART THREE

Paperwork

CHAPTER 20

The Best (and Worst) Deals in a Home Improvement Loan

D o you have a remodeling project in mind? A job that really needs to be done, that will improve the look of your home now and make it irresistible to the next buyer?

Sounds perfect. Do you know where the money to pay for it will come from? Oh, you're still thinking about that part of it.

Actually, you have many sources of home improvement loans for projects as large as a new addition to the house or as small (relatively) as insulation—sources that can offer quite affordable interest rates, as well as other benefits. Some of them may surprise you.

What's Involved Here

There are a couple of important points to keep in mind as you consider this aspect of home improvement.

Don't borrow unless you have to. Loans cost money, even those offering the most advantageous terms. If you have the cash, use it. An exception might be if using your own money cleans out an emergency fund. Another would be a government-sponsored loan for your improvement. If you can secure one at a low interest rate—say, four or five percent—then you might opt to leave your savings in a mutual fund where you are drawing more.

Get estimates of the work you will need done before seeking the loan. Commercial lenders will probably require that you bring in three estimates so they can be sure you are not overpaying for an improvement. *You* can use those documents to get an idea of what the project will cost so you don't borrow more than you need.

Searching for Loan Sources

You might ask relatives for a loan if it is a fairly small amount you will need (or unless they are *very* well positioned to lend you any amount at all). You probably realize there is a certain amount of psychological baggage you will be carrying around until that money is repaid.

If you have a whole life insurance policy, you may be able to borrow against it. The face value of the policy is, of course, reduced by the amount of the loan. You can make up the borrowed amount by increasing your regular payments.

Check with your broker if you own securities to see about borrowing in that area, which might be better for you than a deal from a commercial lender.

If you belong to an employee credit union, look into its terms too. Credit unions have always been an excellent loan source for members.

Is your contractor offering you an improvement loan? Home improvement scams extend to financing, so watch yourself here. There have been homeowners who signed loan papers with a contractor not knowing they were signing for a second mortgage or home equity loan at terms they could not afford. Your best bet is to deal directly with a bank or other mortgage lender, instead of with the contractor for financing.

Finally in this section, you can look to unsecured home improvement loans offered by commercial lenders. Terms and amounts vary from one institution to another, but for the most part you can expect to be able to borrow $15,000 to $20,000 for five or 10 years at a rate of interest likely to be higher than the prevailing one.

With this type of loan, you do not offer your home as collateral. You are judged for eligibility solely on your ability to pay (income, job and credit history), just as you would be in buying a house or car. This is where you can expect to be asked for the written estimates, a detailed outline of the project, and have a contractor lined up too. The interest on these loans is not tax deductible.

Some Little-Known Lenders

There are many sources that lend money to smart homeowners year after year, but a sizable number of people know little or nothing about them. Too bad. There can be some good borrowing terms here, especially with those offered by the government.

If you are planning an energy-saving installation such as storm windows or insulation, check with your local utility company. Many offer low-interest (or no-interest) loans for those purchases. There are no income requirements, although there can be a ceiling for the amount borrowed that is usually around $5,000. Householders 65 or older may find utilities offering special programs directed at them.

Robert Berko of the Consumer Education Research Center, a New Jersey–based nonprofit organization, is the coauthor, with Monroe Speigel of "Consumers Guide to Home Repair Grants and Subsidized Loans" (available for $12.95 plus $3.00 shipping and handling from CERC Grants, 350 Scotland Road, Orange, NJ 07050, or by calling 800-USA-0121 with a credit card order).

To Berko, it is amazing how few people head for their local utility company or other agencies eager to hand out money.

"Some of these programs have no income ceilings," Berko points out, "and others allow incomes of as much as $100,000 per year. There are even some programs or grants for people who are poor credit risks." He recalled that a man who had worked on the book "received a $5,000 New Jersey grant, plus a $4,000 interest-free loan from his utility company. In many areas, people with disabilities can receive grants to pay for needed repairs such as access ramps and widening of doorways."

To learn about federal government loans, you can call your regional office of the U.S. Department of Housing and Urban Development (HUD), listed in the telephone book under US Government.

A popular loan source is the Title 1 program of the Federal Housing Administration (FHA) where that agency insures loans made by private lenders. Title 1 lets you borrow up to $25,000 with a payback period as long as 20 years. You can borrow less but if the amount you need is more than $5,000 the debt must be secured by a lien against your home, so it is considered a mortgage debt. That would bring a tax deduction for the interest you pay. The interest charged with a

Title 1 loan is likely to be higher than for a home equity loan (coming up next), but lower than a commercial lender's home improvement loan.

You can call HUD's national number, 800-733-4663, for the names of local lenders administering Title 1 loans.

Some government-sponsored loans are strictly local, just for a particular city or even limited to a certain section of a town. They are offered to upgrade specific neighborhoods and all homeowners living within those borders can qualify. You might contact your local community development agency, listed in the phone book under your city government's offices, to see what programs are available where you live.

Borrowing Against Your Home

Your choices here are refinancing your home loan or securing a second mortgage or home equity loan. The advantage to any of them is that the interest you pay is tax deductible, whereas most other loan programs are considered consumer debt, with no tax deductions allowed. The disadvantage is that your home is on the line, since you now have your first mortgage plus this new loan payment to make each month.

All call for up-front costs. But shop around. Many lenders offer special terms, advertising from time to time "No points!" or even "No closing costs!"

The home equity loan, which has become increasingly popular with homeowners over the last few years, and which might be *the* most popular choice for a home improvement loan, comes in two forms—a line of credit or a second mortgage.

Broadly speaking, lines of credit are adjustable rate loans, while second mortgages carry fixed interest rates. The second mortgage is popular when fixed rates are low. The line of credit, usually priced somewhat below the second mortgage (at least at the beginning), becomes preferable in periods of higher rates.

A line of credit has another plus that could work well for you. Once you are approved, you can draw on your equity by writing a check or using a credit card only as you need it. You pay interest only on the amount you borrow. The second mortgage comes to you in a lump sum and you pay interest on the entire sum. With some equity lines you can draw on your equity over and over without having to be approved for a new loan and paying the accompanying closing costs.

Of course, you must have enough equity in your home to secure one of these loans. Most lenders will let you borrow from 70 to 80 percent of your home's current value, less the amount of your outstanding mortgage.

Refinancing a first mortgage was enormously popular in 1993 as interest rates fell to their lowest level in 20 or 25 years. There seemed to be almost a contest among lenders to see how low rates could go. That flurry is past now as interest rates have begun another slow climb, although with occasional drops of a fraction of a percentage point or so. If you are still paying fairly high interest and can refinance to one at least two points lower, then by all means consider doing so. The money you draw out for your home improvement can be spread out over the life of the loan. Refinancing does, however, call for closing costs—points, possibly, an appraisal fee, new title insurance policy, etc.—that can add another three to five percent to the cost of your loan if you are not able to secure some concessions from a lender.

If you have already refinanced to the lowest possible interest rate, you might want to go with the line of credit or second mortgage, whichever offers the best terms considering the state of the economy at the time you are loan-shopping.

Don't Bother with Credit Cards

Tapping your credit cards for the money for a home improvement is a poor choice. With interest rates at 17 to 19 percent, you will be paying off that loan forever. You can surely find more agreeable terms with one of the sources mentioned above. Decent loan terms can help you better enjoy that improvement you've made, too.

S U M M I N G   U P

$ Pay cash if you can. That will cost you the least.

$ Look to your utility company and to federal and local govern-
ment agencies for little-known programs with good borrowing
terms.

$ Shop around at lending institutions. All have different rates—
and different promotional programs that can mean better terms
for you.

$ Remember with loans tied to the equity in your home, you now
have essentially two mortgages to pay.

CHAPTER 21

How a Reverse Mortgage Can Increase Retirement Income

Are you at least 62 years of age? Can you use more money? Then you might want to look into obtaining a *reverse mortgage*, also known as a reverse annuity mortgage (RAM).

What's Involved Here

This is a loan that allows homeowners to draw on the equity in their houses without selling the property. That equity can be retrieved as a cash lump sum, in monthly installments, a line of credit or perhaps a combination of those methods. The line of credit is especially popular, since it gives retirees a "cushion" of money available for needed home repairs to pay medical bills not covered by insurance or for any emergency.

It is called a reverse mortgage because that is exactly how it operates. Instead of the homeowner making a payment to the lender each month, the lender pays the homeowner. Also unlike conventional home loans, the reverse mortgage adds on interest and servicing fees at the end of the loan, not up front. The total amount of principal, interest, closing costs, monthly service charges and any other costs become due when the homeowner sells, moves or dies.

The heirs of those who choose this loan can pay it off by refinancing it into a regular mortgage or by using the proceeds from the sale of the home. If the heirs choose to turn the loan into a mortgage, they must qualify for such a loan.

If you are interested in this source of added retirement income, the amount you will be eligible to borrow is usually based on your age, the equity in your home and the interest rate the lender is charging. In most cases you can draw on sixty to eighty percent of your home's appraised value, an amount that protects the lender in case property values drop during the loan term.

There are no income requirements for borrowers. It is your home that is the focus of attention, not you (aside from your age).

The money you receive is nontaxable, since it is considered proceeds from a loan and not income. It does not affect your Social Security or Medicare benefits.

You still own your home and remain responsible for paying taxes and insurance and handling repairs and maintenance.

You cannot lose your home with a reverse mortgage unless it is for a reason any homeowner might: not making mortgage payments, not paying real estate taxes, etc.

"Some people use these loans to get out of a delinquent mortgage or home equity loan situation that was going into foreclosure," says Ken Scholen, director of the nonprofit National Center for Home Equity Conversion. "Then they don't have any more monthly payments."

Here are some numbers to help you see this type of loan in a human context—who is making use of reverse mortgages and for how much income.

The results of an evaluation of an experimental program from the U.S. Department of Housing and Urban Development (HUD), released in 1992, found that nearly three-quarters of the 2,100 borrowers studied chose totally or in part to go with the line of credit selection of a reverse mortgage.

The median age of borrowers, the study found, was 76. Their homes had a median value of $103,000 and the median monthly payment to them was $401. Their median income was $7,600. Interestingly, some 75 percent of those studied had no children, so there was no need to consider passing the home on free and clear to heirs.

There are many plans under the reverse mortgage umbrella. Some call for fixed-rate interest, others adjustable rates. (The interest is not deductible for income tax purposes until you pay off all or part of the total reverse mortgage debt.) Other plans, called "portables," allow homeowners to continue collecting payments even if they move out of their houses.

Reverse mortgages began appearing in the mid-to-late 1980s, and have caught on very slowly. There used to be very few lenders offering them, but the loans have grown in popularity over the last two or three years as word spreads. Estimates place their number at around 20,000 to date. While they are not available at every mortgage lender in town, they can be obtained without as much difficulty as there was even five years ago. The Federal Housing Administration now also insures the loans, which is more proof of retirees' growing interest in this source of income.

Another indicator: a spokesperson for the American Association of Retired Persons said AARP receives more requests for information on reverse mortgages—75,000 in 1993 alone—than on any other topic (there is more about how AARP can help you with reverse mortgages at the end of the this chapter). AARP has encouraged the development and refining of reverse mortgage programs to allow senior citizens who are house rich but cash poor to remain in their homes.

To locate a RAM lender in your area, you can call your local HUD office, listed in the telephone book under U.S. Government.

The National Center for Home Equity Conversion (NCHEC) offers a very helpful, 350-page book called *Retirement Income on the House* that comes with a list of lenders that offer reverse mortgages. For the lender list and the book, send $29.45 (includes shipping and handling), to NCHEC, Suite 115, 7373 147th St. W., Apple Valley, MN 55124, or call 800-247-6553. If you are a member of AARP, you can cut that price in half.

Drawbacks?

Yes, there are a few.

- You cannot leave your house free and clear to your heirs unless you have paid off the loan.
- It *is* expensive. There is interest on the loan. There are closing costs that can run to several thousand dollars the way they do

with a traditional mortgage, and service fees each month, too, ranging from $30 to $50 (added to the end of the loan).
- You should expect to remain in your home for at least five years, or you can find the costs of one of these loans too steep to be worthwhile.

Or Consider This

Besides the reverse mortgage, another way of draining needed cash from your home is to sell it, invest the proceeds and rent an apartment or a house. The interest from that investment can be your extra income. Work the numbers to determine the wiser strategy of the two.

More Information

Naturally, you will want to learn more before approaching a lender for this type of loan. Several sources stand ready to help.

Besides the material from NCHEC, there is "Home-Made Money," offered by the American Association of Retired Persons. Write AARP Home Equity Conversion Information Center, American Association of Retired Persons, 601 E St. NW, Washington, DC 20049, or call 800-424-3410.

The Federal Trade Commission, Public Reference Branch, 6th St. and Pennsylvania Ave. NW, Washington, DC 20580, will send the free brochure "Facts for Consumers—Reverse Mortgages."

You should also discuss the loan with your financial planner, attorney or other professional adviser. Yes, talk with your children, too. Interestingly, besides the HUD study, another group conducted a small survey asking children's reaction to the reverse mortgage, since it can cut into the parents' estates. The children were enthusiastic. The loan often allowed parents to remain in the home they wanted and permitted them to remain independent. That was what mattered to the children.

SUMMING UP

$ A reverse mortgage can supply you with needed cash, every month or through a line of credit, to supplement retirement income.

$ There are many different kinds of loans available here, as there are with primary mortgages, so it is necessary to bone up on and analyze what is being offered.

$ Talk over your plans with a professional adviser and with your children.

CHAPTER 22

Challenging Your Property Tax Bill— And Winning

Property taxes cause many homeowners major headaches. When they remain at their current high level (almost all homeowners feel they are paying too much), that sizable expense is annoying and frustrating. When taxes rise, sometimes spiraling dramatically, another element is added to that mixture: disgust.

You gotta pay your taxes. But maybe you and your local government can agree on a lower figure than the one you are reading on your current tax bill. More homeowners are challenging their bills, fed up with steadily rising taxes, often with a corresponding decline in services. Many times they are winning.

What's Involved Here

Property tax monies are needed by local government for fire and police services, schools and the general running of the community. Fair enough, you say. But why does the amount I pay have to make such sizable jumps each year? Why is the fellow down the street paying a $2,000 tax for his home, which seems identical to mine, and I'm slapped with a $3,500 bill? Why am I paying rising taxes when homes here have been depreciating in recent years? What gives here?

You can challenge your property tax bill. Interestingly, about half the people who appeal a bill succeed in winning a reduction of at least 10 percent. So you stand an even chance your time will not be wasted.

Procedures and formulas for assessing and setting tax rates, a little-known part of local government, vary from one community to the next. What you will be attempting to do is change the *assessment* on your home. You cannot appeal the tax rate, which is set by law.

Two Tales of Tough Taxes

When Mike Flanagan moved to his brand-new Colorado home from another part of the country two years ago, he was handed a tax bill based on a house assessed at $245,000. He had just paid $228,000 for the property.

Flanagan headed downtown. The appeal, he recalls, "was a visit to the appraiser's office. The whole process took 10 minutes." Flanagan's house was reassessed at $228,000. Houses there are assessed at their selling price, so there was no great amount of work to be done. Flanagan's new property tax bill reflected a $300-a-year reduction from the one he originally received.

"Where I lived in the East," he said with a laugh, "that would have involved a process of confrontation and wouldn't have been handled anywhere near as expeditiously."

That's one way, and certainly a painless one, to see your taxes lowered.

When the government ordered a reevaluation of the homes in Claudia Logue's small northeastern city in the late 1980s, for the first time in 16 or 17 years, homeowners held their collective breath. At that time houses, most of which were selling for $150,000 to $400,000, were carrying assessment figures of around $20,000 to $40,000.

Real estate taxes were already high in that aging community, which had a continual budget deficit and need for more money in its coffers. How much higher could they go?

"I was going to have to pay around $7,500," Logue recalls. "I had already been paying $5,000."

Residents' vocal outrage forced city government to make more than the usual low-key arrangements to plead a tax bill. Special offices were set up all over town and they were crowded with cranky taxpayers, waiting to point out inconsistencies in the reevaluation process. Logue's contention, when she went to the temporary setup nearest her, was that the assessor saw only one-third of her house during the door-to-door reevaluation. He looked at her floor-through apartment, but said he did not need to see her tenant's duplex, which she said had not been remodeled and was not in keeping with her renovated floor. Unfair!

So many inaccuracies were found in that reevaluation that city government let go the company that had conducted it and hired a new one. Everyone went through the process again and this time taxes rose but not to the height they would have reached with the original reevaluation.

How You Can Get a Lower Tax Bill

You can do it yourself, like Mike Flanagan. Or you can adopt the strength-in-numbers approach of Claudia Logue and her fellow homeowners (although they had to prepare their cases and do their own individual homework). What you should *not* do is rush into the appropriate taxing office screaming, "Look at this bill. This is obscene. I shouldn't have to . . ." and on and on and on.

It should be said, too, that perhaps the taxes you are asked to pay are quite in line with others in your town.

There are two ways you can get your bill lowered, however. One is if there is a mistake in your file. Your house is listed as having 2,300 square feet, for instance, when it actually has 1,300 square feet. Or the value of your land is listed higher than other lots in your neighborhood.

If you can claim your tax bill is out of line with your neighbors' houses you might be successful, too. What you must show here is how very similar your properties are in lot size, square feet and number of bedrooms and baths. You must be comparing apples with apples.

You might want to pay for an independent appraisal to strengthen your case.

None of the above should be confused with heading for the tax office if you have not received a tax break you are due, such as those allowed for the elderly. In those instances the problem is likely to be quickly resolved, with no elaboration needed of your case.

How do you handle a full-fledged tax appeal?

- Pay close attention not only to your tax bill but also to the tax assessment notice that is usually mailed in the spring and fall. If you want to protest your taxes, this is what you will be disputing. The notice will probably state that if you want to complain, you have *x* number of days or weeks to do so. Then it will tell you where to report if you want to enter a protest. You can talk with the assessor, or lodge a formal appeal with the local board of tax review.
- Call the assessor's office to see what it offers in the way of printed material explaining the setting of real estate taxes and how homeowners can challenge them. Ask staffers there if other protests have been filed, especially if there has just been a reevaluation and this is the first tax bill after new assessment figures have been released.
- Visit the assessor's office to review others' taxes and see if yours are in line with what they are paying. This is all a matter of public record, with no secrecy involved.
- If you do not have the time or the inclination to pursue this yourself, you can hire someone to seek a tax reduction for you. In Claudia Logue's town, after the reevaluation, one or two companies in town that offered appraising services advertised that they would help individual homeowners appeal for a new tax bill for a fee of around $150. In your town you might have a property tax consultant. Or you can ask a real estate agent to refer you to one.

    You can also write for the pamphlet "How to Fight Property Taxes," published by the National Taxpayers' Union. Send $2 to their office at 325 Pennsylvania Ave. SE, Washington, DC 20003.

There is one point you might want to keep in the back of your mind during this process: if you do *not* have a solid case and are causing quite a stir, you might end up calling attention to yourself and perhaps learn you are underassessed and undertaxed! That's why it's so important to prepare before a meeting at your assessor's office or appearance before a tax board.

If you *are* prepared, secure (and perhaps a bit smug) in the knowledge that you are in the right and can prove it, you are likely to be rewarded with a tax cut that can put quite a few dollars back into the old bank account. Keep monitoring your assessment and tax statements, though. Mistakes can crop up again.

SUMMING UP

💲 You can protest on your own or join a tax revolt in your community. Both will require homework on your part.

💲 The tax records you will be looking for are at your assessor's office and are open to anyone.

💲 Be sure you are comparing your home with one that is almost exactly like yours and in the same neighborhood.

💲 You might find it more practical to hire someone to pursue this for you.

CHAPTER 23

How To Save on Insurance

Insurance for your home? Many of us do not like to think about it.

Still, over the last few years the natural disasters around the country—hurricanes, tornadoes, fires, floods and earthquakes—have shown, in heart-wrenching pictures, how little control we have over outside forces that can change our lives and ruin our homes.

In 1992 the *National Underwriter*, an insurance trade journal, estimated that 67 percent of the nation's homes lacked adequate insurance. The journal based that figure on a study that showed the main problems resulted from homeowners passing on incorrect information to the insurance company at the outset, with years going by and no one correcting that data. Also, there was no updating of changes to a house, such as a remodeled kitchen or expensive electronic gear purchased over the years.

Guess we really *don't* want to think about it.

Guess you can see why we should.

Does that mean you ought to run out and buy whatever is on the shelves? Not at all. In fact, you can still save—and quite a bit, too—on what you have now in the way of protection and what you need to buy for additional peace of mind.

What's Involved Here

First, it is a good idea to get out all your insurance policies—home, auto, medical and life. Check to be sure you are adequately covered and if not, how much more coverage you need and in what areas. But you also ought to check for duplication or overlapping of coverage, which is costing you money.

This book is about your home. So this chapter will concern itself with policies about those protection choices. Incidentally, if you are a condominium owner, you will carry a special policy protecting the interior of your apartment while the condo association pays for insurance for the exterior of the apartments and other building, and grounds. You will find many of the tips and suggestions in this chapter apply to you too.

Homeowners Insurance

Since you probably have a mortgage on your home—only a small percentage of owners pay cash, and another small number have paid off their home loans—then you already have a homeowners insurance policy. No getting around it, virtually all mortgage lenders require it. The average $100,000 house will cost around $400 a year in insurance premiums, but the cost can vary rather widely among carriers, taking into account the amount of coverage the homeowner chooses.

You hold one of a small variety of homeowner protections, each differing slightly from the other, but all essentially covering your house in the event of damage from fire, smoke, lightning, theft and vandalism, windstorm or hailstorm. (Yes, you are also covered for that rather new and bizarre phenomenon, the sinkhole.)

That same policy also offers liability protection and covers your personal property at 50 percent of the replacement cost of your home (if it is replacement cost you are carrying). And perhaps you have special riders for protection beyond what the homeowners policy provides, for jewelry, antiques, furs and silverware.

Replacement Value

Homeowners used to be urged to purchase insurance at 80 percent of replacement value of their home. But the storms, fires and other calamities of the last few years have shown it is no longer such a remote possibility that a house can be totally destroyed. Replacement value is what it would cost to rebuild your home today, versus cash value coverage, which is the amount it would take to repair or replace damage after subtracting depreciation due to use. You pay the difference between replacement cost and depreciated cost.

Cash value coverage is not recommended, and now, instead of 80 percent replacement coverage, you are advised today to carry 100 replacement cost coverage, which will pay for rebuilding your home with materials of similar kind and quality as those used originally.

What you want here is a *guaranteed replacement cost* policy. Interestingly, to the insurer, replacement cost is not likely to include any expenses for complying with building code standards of today that did not exist when the house was built, even if that was just a few years ago. Some insurers offer endorsements to a homeowners policy that will pay toward that cost, at a $100 or so annual fee. Go for it.

Very old and historic houses are considered later in these pages.

Saving on Spending/Saving Your Home

Here are some suggestions for spending you may not have considered, with the thought that buying some types of coverage might save you a greater expense in the event of serious problems or outright disaster affecting your home. There are several ways to cut costs on your homeowners policy, too, some of them not reducing coverage at all.

- An obvious suggestion: shop around for the best coverage at the best price, the way you would for automobile insurance. Companies' rates *do* vary. Just be certain, when looking over what everyone has to offer, you are comparing rates for identical coverage. If your mortgage lender pays your homeowner insurance premiums for you and you want to change carriers, simply advise your lender of your new insurer.
- If the premiums quoted are more than you can afford right now, instead of not carrying the insurance at all, raise the deductible (the amount you will have to pay yourself in the event of loss). If need be, you can probably absorb a small sum that is not covered.
- Using the same carrier for both automobile and homeowners insurance can cut premium costs with some companies. You

can save as much as 20 percent on your homeowners coverage and 15 percent off your auto premium.

- Pay your insurance premium annually, instead of quarterly or monthly, to save service charges.
- Yes, 100 percent replacement coverage for your home is recommended. To save money, however, and if you live in a rather placid area of the country (so far), you might want to go with that 80 percent coverage, thereby slicing about 20 percent from your premium payments. That would leave you paying 20 percent of the cost in the event your home needed total rebuilding. You might want to take that chance since most homeowners are far more likely to file smaller claims—a kitchen destroyed, say—than one that would take in the entire 100 percent of coverage or the whole house in ruins. It's your call.
- Homeowners policies also include liability coverage in the event, for instance, a guest in your home is injured. You might talk to your insurer and ask if you can drop the liability side of your coverage and instead opt for an "umbrella liability policy." This excellent coverage will bring you $1 million to $2 million in protection for a number of mishaps that can befall you and others for a cost of around $120 a year. (Ask your insurer, too, how umbrella coverage can cut your auto insurance premiums.)
- Standard policies also cover personal property. If you choose to be reimbursed for the *depreciated* cost of the damaged or stolen goods, you can save more money in premiums than if you select *replacement* cost. The lower rate will not be enough to replace exactly what you have lost through a major fire or theft, but if you do not mind taking that risk, you can save on premiums.
- Have you made substantial improvements to your home over the last few years without updating your policy? Add to your coverage accordingly, but be careful not to overinsure. You do not need to consider the value of the land, which is not taken into account in homeowners coverage because it is not destroyed by fire, hurricane, etc. You also need not cover the value of such fireproof parts of the building as the foundation.
- If you have a very old, or especially a historic, house you might have to buy modified replacement cost insurance. It is unlikely an insurer is going to guarantee replacing features and details of a house that are virtually impossible to duplicate today.

If you have a hard time finding coverage, don't shrug and drop the subject. Some companies around the country *will* insure the old house as well as offer coverage to those who have filed what the companies see as excessive claims and those who have filed for bankruptcy. For information about these carriers, you can call the Insurance Information Institute at 800-942-4242. Historic house owners can also contact the Washington, DC–based National Trust for Historic Preservation (202-673-4000) for assistance.

These special coverages might carry higher premiums than run-of-the-mill policies.

- If you have difficulty securing insurance with a private policy or are offered what you consider insufficient coverage, perhaps because you live in certain city neighborhoods or live in a disaster-prone area, ask an insurance company about pool coverage. Usually there is some program—federal crime insurance, for example, which is available in nine states and the District of Columbia—where the government or a group of private insurers offers a program for those who have a problem securing insurance where they are.

- A good argument for checking your policy every year or so: some policies offer an "inflation guard" with their coverage that will automatically update your coverage. "Usually they're optional," says Loretta Worters of the Insurance Information Institute, an industry group. "It depends on the company. Some automatically update, but with others you have to ask for the inflation guard." There is a small charge for that protection.

  A small caution here. Yes, it is a good idea to review your coverage periodically to be sure it is up to date. But monitor the numbers in those inflation guard increases, since inflation has been running at a low figure over the last several years.

- Earthquake coverage—and if the E word makes you, excuse the expression, shake, then you are probably in a locale where you need that protection—does not come with the standard homeowners policy. You can buy that needed protection for a few hundred dollars a year—about $300 for a $300,000 house.

- Reimbursement in the event of a flood is also not covered by a homeowners policy, which comes as a dreadful surprise to many homeowners who turn to their policy expecting to be covered after that disaster. Sometimes lenders require flood insurance for houses in certain flood areas of a community.

If no flood coverage under homeowners policies is a fact not known to many homeowners, the federal government's National Flood Insurance Program, administered by the Federal Emergency Management Agency (FEMA) has been an equally dark secret. Or it was until the 1993 floods in the Midwest brought the nation's attention to the lack of coverage for many homeowners there and FEMA's role in offering protection.

If you think you can be in danger from flooding where you are, contact FEMA at 800-638-6620 for information about flood coverage. The agency also offers the free booklet, "Answers to Questions About the National Flood Insurance Program."

While the insurance is a government program, it can be obtained through insurance agents.

- Speaking of catastrophes, you should know that the typical homeowners policy, while it offers protection against windstorms, might not cover your house in the event of a really big blow such as a hurricane. In Florida, for example, residents of the states coastal communities can buy special hurricane coverage at a low annual cost. Look into that specialty in your area if it is hurricane-prone. The money spent for coverage can save you thousands if you are forced to absorb a sizable chunk of the rebuilding yourself.
- Own a brand-new house? Ask about a break in premiums of anywhere from 5 to 20 percent that some companies offer customers whose dwellings are less than five years old.
- If you raise the amount of your policy deductible from the customary low $250 to $500, you will save about 10 percent in premium rates. Take a $1,000 deductible and you will save even more. Just be sure you can afford to absorb smaller claims yourself in the event of loss.
- Have you been a faithful customer of your insurer for several years? Some companies offer discounts to customers who have held policies with them for three to five years.
- If you have installed safety systems such as smoke detectors or dead bolt locks, you can earn a discount on your premiums of about 10 percent.
- If you have added a central-station-reporting fire or burglar alarm, you can slice off another 5 to 10 percent.
- Are you retired? Inquire about a discount that can run as high as 10 percent on your premium payment. The reasoning behind this is that, since most home burglaries occur between 10 AM

and 4 PM, and you are assumed to be at home during the day, your house stands less chance of a break-in.
- Here are some more sources of help when you are puzzled about coverage. Your state insurance department offers printed material about special riders or policies in your area, which can be invaluable when considering insurance purchases. You can also call the National Insurance Consumer Helpline at 800-942-4242 from 8 AM to 8 PM EST, Monday through Friday. They can answer questions, but they steer away from specific companies' rates or ratings.

For the Record

Taking inventory of your home and its possessions can be vitally important in helping the claims process should a loss occur. It can also be valuable to law enforcement officials in recovering those items in the event of theft. Loretta Worters of the Insurance Information Institute, says the most common problem she has seen in the last few years of fires, earthquakes and floods and tornadoes is in this area.

"People do not take inventory of their personal possessions," she notes, "and having that helps expedite their claim. Nobody keeps receipts anymore; that's not realistic. But homeowners should have some record of their valuables, whether it's photos or a video or something on paper."

You can use an instant camera for an inventory, or a camcorder. Just walk through your place, shooting the interior of your home, with valuables visible, perhaps laid out on the bed if they are normally out of view. On the back of the pictures or on a separate sheet of paper, list serial or model numbers, purchase date and price and present value of the items if you know it. Attach what receipts you have.

You can also buy an inventory sheet from a stationer's store or call the Insurance Information Institute at 800-942-4242 for the free form it offers.

When you have your inventory completed, store it in a safety-deposit box or with your insurer or in your own office that is away from home—any safe place away from where it could be destroyed along with the items it is documenting.

Mortgage Insurance

There is, first of all, mortgage *protection* insurance, which advertises itself as continuing to pay your home loan for 6 to 12 months in the event you are laid off. This costs quite a bit, however, for slim coverage in return.

There is also mortgage *life* insurance, which pays off your mortgage in the event of your death. This is not such a good idea either. You will do better with term life insurance, which should be more than enough if your heirs want to pay off your home loan. Mortgage life insurance will cost around $30 a month on a $100,000 loan.

An exception might be made here. If you can get no other insurance protection, perhaps for health reasons, and you want to be sure your family can continue living in your home, then you might want to purchase a mortgage life insurance policy.

SUMMING UP

$ Review your insurance coverage frequently. You may have made major improvements to your home or have valuable new purchases that need special protection. On the other hand, you may no longer need special coverage for, say, the fur coat you sold a few years ago.

$ Shop around for the best rates for the best coverage. All insurers do not charge the same.

$ Look into special protection against floods and earthquakes if they occur in your area. Your standard homeowners policy will not be enough to protect you from these calamities.

$ Have some sort of inventory of your possessions for insurers and, if called for, the police.

CHAPTER 24

Moving On: Getting the Best Price When You Sell

Now, after you have drained every possible dollar from your home, comes the point in your homeowning life that can bring the biggest windfall of all: you are selling and moving on.

Individual life situations vary and economic times have more than a little input in the residential real estate market. But, generally speaking, we sell our homes for more than we paid for them, even if only a little bit more. So how can you get the most for your place, since the most here stands to be not just a few hundred, or even a few thousand, but several thousands of those delectable bits of green paper?

What's Involved Here

First, give some thought to your reason for moving. If it is the result of a job transfer that you want to accept, then of course you must sell.

If you are moving because you want to live in a different neighborhood, perhaps one that is closer to where you work now, then you too are probably set to get your show on the road.

For Pat Burns, early retirement from her position with the state of New Jersey was just one reason for her selling the home she had lived in for more than 40 years.

Burns says she knew when it was time to go. "Property values in my neighborhood were going down and taxes were going up," she recalls. "And with retirement, I wanted a total change. I was very enthusiastic about selling and I never looked back." Burns' move was a positive one and she is now enjoying a brand-new townhouse in a small community a few miles from her old neighborhood.

Indeed, all the reasons Burns cites are good ones for moving. But if you want a larger or smaller house and feel you have to change addresses to accomplish that, then wait a minute. Perhaps you have some money-saving choices here.

If you like your present house and the neighborhood, but you are rattling around in a too-big home, consider converting part of it into a rental apartment. That will not only allow you to stay in the house, saving you the expense of moving, but also will bring in a welcome monthly income. Chapter 7 goes into this option in greater detail.

Stay Put and Remodel

But what if your home is too *small?* Maybe your family has grown since you bought the house, and you now have more small children or grown children moving back to stay with you or parents moving in. Perhaps adding on to your existing home can solve your space problem.

Moving, no matter how you try to keep costs down, *is* expensive.

The house you buy is likely to carry a higher price tag than the one you are in now. There is the real estate agent's fee for selling your present home, closing costs on the new house, moving expenses and the raft of other bills that go along with setting up shop in a new place.

If you could build, say, a bedroom and bath onto your house, would that solve your problem? If you can't add on at the ground level, perhaps you can find the extra space you need by adding a room or two to the top of the house.

Or is it a really large, sun-filled kitchen that has you dreaming and looking at new-home advertisements? Perhaps you could "bump out" your existing room and have your kitchen/sun space, and rather effortlessly too.

If you can create the space you need with some creative remodeling, then turn to Chapter 1. It talks about getting permission to build from local authorities, whether your addition will be in scale with the rest of the neighborhood, what improvements pay back the owner or at least make the home easier to sell when that time comes and whether what you are considering might be money poorly spent.

Nope, Still Want To Move?

Does none of the above apply to you and you just want to get going?

After you have decided where to buy next, which almost every seller knows, at least as far as the town preferred, before hanging up the "For Sale" sign you will have to think about the many steps leading up to replacing that with a "Sold" sign.

You are now taking off the hat of homeowner and putting on the one marked "marketing director." You and only you know the most about your house, its splendid features and unbeatable living style. It is up to you to secure the best price possible. The dollars in clear profit you make can be enough to swing a much nicer house the next time around and can even hand you a nice chunk of money for retirement and/or investment.

It all rests with you.

Your first decision, after making the big one to get going, is whether to sell the house yourself or hire a realty salesperson to do it for you.

Selling It Yourself

Let's see, you figure, this house is worth $180,000. If we sell it at that price through a real estate agent, we'll have to pay six percent, or $10,800.

Wow! Wouldn't it be great to save *that* chunk of money?

Sure would. That is why some 20 percent of homeowners sell their homes themselves these days.

By all means, give it a try. There are any number of books on the market now to guide you through the do-it-yourself selling process.

"If the real estate inventory is low where you are," says Carolyn Janik, "and there are not as many listings as the real estate agency would like, then that's the time to do it yourself."

Janik, a real estate agent and the author of several real estate books, including *How To Sell Your Home in the 90s* (Viking, $10.95), cautions against doing it *all* yourself. "There are so many problems that could come up," she points out, "that a sales contract might get messy. You can buy these contracts in a stationery store, but my suggestion is have a good lawyer draw it up for you."

Keep in mind if you do want to sell your home on your own you must be very enthusiastic about taking on that responsibility, because you will be very busy. You must screen calls about the house, show prospects through, negotiate over price, monitor the buyer's mortgage application process, deal with the house inspector and more. The lawyer will help with the contract and the closing, but that still leaves a number of substantial details that are your responsibility.

The two most common reasons Fizbo (FSBO, or for sale by owner) deals do not work out are (1) not enough buyers seeing the property or making an offer and (2) the house is priced too high and the seller is inflexible about negotiating. Indeed, reason number 1 might be the result of reason number 2.

Be sure you price *your* home wisely if you are selling it yourself (and even if you work with an agent, although a professional real estate associate will likely bring you down to earth about your expectations).

An appraisal can help you determine a figure. So can the selling price of homes in your immediate neighborhood. They are a matter of public record and many newspapers publish selling prices weekly. Keep in mind how your home differs from those being sold, so you can zero in on a price tag for your place that is most likely to lead to success.

When Joyce and Bob Fitzpatrick moved from Wisconsin to their retirement home in the South, Joyce Fitzpatrick remembered that a house down the street had recently been sold

"That house was practically identical to ours," she says, "except we spent $3,000 to have a 12-foot-by-24-foot closed-in porch built at the rear of ours. So we set our asking price $5,000 above what they got."

Ask a few thousand dollars more than selling prices in your locale to allow for negotiating, the way the Fitzpatricks did, and you should be on target. A run-down, dirty house will turn off buyers, but at least it can be cleaned up and a sale price agreed upon based on the mess. But the seller of a property who has priced it too high and is determined not to budge, is on the way to selling failure. Be reasonable, be flexible.

If 20 percent of homeowners sell their houses on their own, the remaining 80 percent must use a real estate agency. If you have not sold your home after a month or six weeks, you might turn to the professionals instead of taking—perhaps wasting—more time doing it yourself. Yes, it will cost you a six percent commission. But the real estate agent might be able to sell the property quickly, and at a better price than you seem to be commanding, by marketing it yourself.

Negotiating, which makes up so much of the selling process, is difficult for most of us who have never sold a home before and who, let's confess, might be a little blind to our home's faults and failings.

The Real Estate Agent

Hiring a real estate salesperson is, for most Americans, the path to selling their home. Interview three agents before selecting one. Ask them: Do you work full-time? (Don't bother with part-timers.) What do you think is the best price for this house? How will you market it? Are you on the Multiple Listing Service? (Most are; stay away from any that are not because your property will not have maximum exposure.) How can this house be improved for a faster, better sale?

Do not necessarily sign with the agent who gives you the highest asking price for your home. He or she might just be trying to get your listing. You should have some sense by now, after talking to realty people and noticing sales in your neighborhood, that a sky-high price is not a wise strategy. Your asking price should be based on "comparables," which is the agency's listing of recently sold homes in your area. All of them should be within a fairly narrow range, which can help you target the right figure for your place.

When you choose one of the three agents, sign an agreement for 60 or 90 days. Agents might put up a fuss over that short span of time, and want your listing for six months, but the shorter term will work better for you. If you are not pleased with the agent after that date, you can change to another one. If you are satisfied with the agent's performance even though your home has not yet sold, you can sign up again with him or her.

Getting Your House in Order

Next to an inflated asking price, the biggest turnoff to house shoppers is a dirty home. A cluttered one is not much better.

If you cannot clean your place within an inch of its life before you begin showing it, perhaps because you both work and there is just no time, do consider hiring a cleaning service, even if just for the first month the house is on the market. That is when it is likely to see the greatest number of potential buyers trooping through. Once the major cleaning is done, you can maintain it yourself. Everything must be spanking clean, not just the obvious kitchen and baths. Walls, woodwork, floors, fixtures—in many homes it's scrub, scrub, scrub for several months before the house is officially announced for sale. Not to mention the daily sweeping, dusting and mopping and bedmaking. At all times the house must look perfect. Yes, it is a chore. But frankly, no one wants to buy someone else's dirt and grime.

Dirt, real estate agents say, is a repugnant turnoff to buyers, but clutter can deep-six a sale too. If buyers cannot see beyond your trophies, family photographs and other bric-a-brac, their eyes will tire and they will move on to the next place. Househunters are not that imaginative, realty agents say. You cannot ask them, for instance, to picture the kitchen counters without all those appliances and dishes and flowerpots. You have to present the picture to them.

The secret here, although it is a tip not confidential at all, is to make your home look like the model homes for sale in your community. Visit some as you begin to perk up your own house for sale. Yes, the models do not look lived in, but that's what buyers want. They want to imagine themselves in that setting, picture their own furniture and, yes, their own family photos and trophies here and there.

So go home after your visit to model homes and sweep kitchen counters clear, leaving, as you have seen in the models, just a vase of fresh flowers or a plant. Clear table tops in the living room and pack away personal accessories, including awards and religious items. Your home will now be as neutral—and inviting—as those brandnew ones on the market.

Should you spend money fixing up your place? Some. But this is not the time for major cash outlays. What's important: attractive landscaping; clean paint, inside and out; no plumbing problems; and nothing broken, from window sashes to a cooling system. Replace the obviously worn and old—window shades, for example—with new and fresh. Buyers *will* notice.

This calls for taking a *very* dispassionate look at your home and having an eagerness to anticipate what buyers are looking for and will expect.

"People can be hesitant to make updates at such a late date," says Sue Solmos, who was an Indianapolis real estate agent until she recently became an independent realty consultant. "They feel 'If it's good enough for me, why isn't it good enough for them?'

"Those sellers probably won't make as much as they could because they're unwilling to make repairs or upgrades."

And Also . . .

When it comes to negotiating over price, as stated above, don't be afraid to come down a little to meet your buyer's offer. Your asking price, after all, took into account a little give and take.

Janik explains one good way to negotiate without giving away too much is to withhold in your listing for your home phrases like "draperies, chandeliers included." Keep out any items of real value and use them as bargaining tools later. For example, take the gap between what you want for your home and what an interested buyer is willing to pay. Say they have offered $235,000 for your home, and will go no higher. You might say "You can have it for $239,000 (or $238,000), and we'll throw in the $4,000 dining room chandelier."

If you are leaving a house for a high-rise apartment building, you can offer the patio furniture in lieu of taking a slightly lower offer. If you will no longer need the baby's room furnishings, you can offer a furnished nursery to would-be buyers expecting their first child. (Be sure the nursery is attractive and nicely furnished, of course.)

Check with your accountant for savings you can realize in moving. A job transfer might bring some tax breaks. Then there is the "55 and over deduction." If you are 55 or older, the Internal Revenue Service will allow an exemption of up to $125,000 in profit from the sale of your home. You or your co-owner spouse must be at least 55 on the day of the sale and must have owned and lived in the house for any three of the five years preceding its sale. Neither of you can have used the exemption previously.

Finally, you can save money by not buying the next home until you have sold your present one. It will be difficult to do this, but it is the wisest financial decision. There is more about the sell-buy situation in the next chapter.

SUMMING UP

$ You can save the greatest amount of money by not moving at all. See if you can remodel to get the features you want.

$ If you want to sell your home yourself, do your homework— and find a good real estate lawyer.

$ Be realistic and flexible in setting your price. Everyone wants to negotiate.

$ Clean, clean, clean. And while you are at it, get rid of clutter.

$ Keep some items out of your home listing to use for bargaining later.

$ Don't buy the next house until you have sold the one you are in now.

CHAPTER 25

Avoiding Financial Calamity When You Sell One House To Buy Another

The dream: selling where you are now and moving into a larger or smaller home, exactly what you have been looking for.

The nightmare: owning two homes simultaneously and carrying two mortgages.

It happens. Timing and money disasters strike many homeowners when they are selling one home to buy another. Some find themselves shackled with simultaneous mortgage payments on two houses or condominiums when they make the switch. Others face several homeless months between the time they move out of their old residence and the time they can move into the new one.

These problems usually stem from the two primary steps involved in changing houses: liquefying your assets (getting the money out of the first house so you can make the down payment on the next) and coordinating your occupancy (the big switch of family and furniture). Here is how to avoid pitfalls, make the most money you can from the sale and the purchase, and save as much as possible during that patch of time before you are safely settled into the home you have bought.

What's Involved Here

The situation you find yourself in is likely to fall into one of the following scenarios.

The Corporate Transfer

If this is why you are moving, congratulations. It is by far the simplest of sell/buy situations—financially, anyway. Most companies offer to buy, at fair market value, the home of their transferred employee; in some cases the company will lend the employee the equity in that home without interest, so there is money for a down payment on the next house, and will manage the property after the family moves. Managing the property usually means maintaining and paying mortgage installments, insurance and taxes until it is sold. Most companies also will pay living expenses while the family househunts and/or awaits closing.

To make it easier on the family in this instance, however, try to buy a vacant resale house, which will allow you to close when *you* want. Even though the company is paying for your temporary lodgings, you want to be in your own place as soon as possible.

Other buying choices that will make the move smooth for you, in descending order: new houses, either complete or on the verge of completion; the homes of other people being transferred and, to a lesser extent, the homes of people who have already bought another property.

Changing Jobs

If you are merely changing jobs and are not selling because your company is transferring you, you will not have as much financial support from the company as the transferee but there might be some assistance. Few companies will buy your home, but most will pay your moving expenses and provide some financial support for living expenses while you await a closing in the new location.

A long-distance job change often separates a family. If some members have stayed behind to sell the old house, the family will want quick occupancy of their new home in order to reunite.

Obviously a person in this position should try to select from the same selling situations recommended to the corporate transferee, avoiding those choices bound to bring delays.

If you are buying the home of a job changer, you can usually expect an on-time closing. Those sellers are both anxious for and in need of equity.

Stepping Up or Stepping Down

When your home no longer fits your needs you will probably opt for a change, moving either to a larger one, or, if that is your dream, a smaller house. Or perhaps a condominium near the city, or a house farther out in the country.

Whatever you prefer, you will be choosing the house you definitely want now.

Try to get a closing date on the house you are buying four to six months ahead if you do not already have a sales contract on the house you are selling. Price your home to sell. There is more about that in the preceding chapter.

It is much easier to wait out the extra time in your old house than it is to make mortgage payments on two properties and a bridge loan. (A bridge loan is a commonly used term for a short-term loan from a lending institution that allows you to make a down payment on the new house before you have in hand the equity from the home you are selling.)

If you are buying a house from sellers who have already bought another home you have a strong negotiating hand. Your first offer should be at a low price with a distant closing date. If you follow that by slight increases in the offering price and offers to close sooner and sooner, you may well save yourself several thousand dollars. Once the contract is signed, however, be prepared to close on time. Sellers who are carrying the payments on two properties might well take steps that would force you, the buyer, to choose between closing on the appointed day and forfeiting all escrow deposits.

Building a New Home

Most builders will tell you they can have a new house ready for occupancy in 90 to 120 days after groundbreaking. Hmmmmm. This is only occasionally the case. And even more rarely can you do anything to speed things up. Actual closing dates usually run one to six months—sometimes even nine months—after the contract date.

If you are selling your old home while having another built allow plenty of time beyond the paper closing date on the new property for the closing on the old. How much time? Talk to some folks who have moved into houses constructed by your builder.

The risk of setting too early a closing date on your old house is that you will have nowhere to move if your new home is not completed. Emotionally, that is enormously stressful. It can cost you a bundle in temporary living expenses and furniture storage, too. In contrast, the risk of setting too late a closing date is that the builder does finish on time and you are forced to take out a bridge loan in order in order to close.

Moving to Another Part of the Country

This is common among retirees, but applies to any home sellers heading for a new place hundreds, perhaps thousands, of miles from where they are now. How can you manage to sell in one place and simultaneously househunt in another at so great a distance?

For many wise long-distance movers, the answer is you don't. Continue having your house on the market in your present community and when it is sold, move into a rental apartment in the new locale, signing a month-by-month, a six-month or, if absolutely necessary, a one-year lease.

The advantages here are several. You are not forced into accepting less for your old house than you want simply because you must get on the road and you are not buying a house in the new community just because it is available and the long-distance mover is practically at your door. Also, the breathing space in the apartment allows you to househunt at a more leisurely pace, looking into all your options, some of which you may not have known existed in your perhaps cursory overview of your new locale.

When Joyce and Bob Fitzpatrick retired from their teaching positions in Wisconsin and moved to the Sun Belt, they rented a three-bedroom townhouse for seven months in the city where they planned to settle.

"Renting gave us time to look around here and there," Bob Fitzpatrick recalls "We spent quite a bit of time driving around the beach areas and the suburbs before we chose to have a home built in what we thought was the best community for us."

Moving Without Selling

Here is another problem: having to move without selling your home first. This can happen when, say, Janet Smith must sell her condominium to marry Jim Jones and move with him to his new assignment in Hong Kong. Perhaps her home has been on the market and has not yet sold; perhaps she will only now put up the For Sale sign and leave the selling to a real estate agent.

The problems here: empty houses do not, as a rule, sell as quickly as those that are furnished and lived in, so the selling process may be delayed even further. Besides the psychological effects of the empty house working against you, with no furniture or draperies or plants to "charm it up," its faults become magnified. Every nail hole in the wall is visible, as is every furniture mark and stain on the carpeting and every faded patch on the wallpaper.

Should Janet rent the house or leave it empty while on the market?

"It depends on Janet's goals and the economic picture (both hers and the nation's) at the time," says Carolyn Janik, a real estate agent and author of several books, including *How To Sell Your Home in the '90s* (Viking, $10.95). "If the mortgage on the condominium is small enough and the maintenance fee low enough to allow for renting at a profit, or at least a break-even cash flow, keeping the apartment for a while may be a good investment. This is especially true if the real estate market is slow in the area. A period of rental may allow for a market recovery and a faster sale at a higher price in the future.

"If renting creates a negative cash flow, however, this seller would probably do better selling the condo vacant. Spending some time and money repainting the interior in neutral tones (the proverbial builder's white is always good) will almost certainly come back tenfold in increased saleability."

Janik adds the same advice applies to a single-family house, but cautions that tenant choice there should be made very carefully because maintenance of the home and yard will depend on that tenant and not, as in Janet's case, on the condominium association.

The Best Sell-Buy Scenario

The very best way to sell your existing home and buy the one you want next is to take it one step at a time. That is, you have a contract from a buyer for your existing home and then you sign a contract to buy your new place.

To pull this off, be sure you keep current with all the properties for sale in your price range in the community you have chosen. Once you are made an acceptable offer for your place, you can in turn make an offer on the best available house and adjust the closing dates on both to your advantage. If you should receive an excellent offer on your old house when there is absolutely nothing on the market that you want to buy, you will need to decide between refusing that offer and accepting it with a request for a distant closing date (four to six months). It's likely that an acceptable property will come on the market during that time. You should know, however, that a buyer can go to court to force a seller to close on his or her property in accordance with the contract, even if the seller has no place to go.

If you are buying a property where the sellers are not certain of their future plans, you may not be able to move in exactly when you choose. Even if you were to get a judgment of specific performance, as it is called, against them, the process could take months. On the other hand, those same sellers might find another house, close on it and move out in plenty of time. This is a difficult one to predict.

Finally. . .

You will, of course, consult your accountant about the tax benefits or bites of this move you plan.

Expect a snag or two when you must sell one home before you buy another. If absolutely everything goes smoothly, rejoice and consider yourself fortunate. The key here is to be rational, informed and as open as possible to new ideas and options—and open to compromise as well.

SUMMING UP

$ Read the preceding chapter again to be sure your house is ready to be put on the market and is priced to sell.

$ In any move where a job is involved—a corporate transfer or simply a new job in a new town—try to get as much help as possible from the company.

$ If you have a choice, do not buy the next house until you have sold the present one.

$ This is a nerve-wracking time for almost all sellers. Try to keep cool in order to make rational, financially sound decisions.

CHAPTER 26

Five More Ideas
To Put Money
in Your Pocket

W e aren't finished. Here are still more ways to put your home to work for you.

A banker said about one of these tips: "More people think about it and talk about it than actually do it. Ninety percent of the people out there are not that disciplined."

Surely he didn't mean *you*.

What's Involved Here

Four of these suggestions call for referring to your mortgage documents and juggling some numbers. But with the fifth, a casual chat might bring you a welcome new monthly income.

Your Mortgage Escrow Account

You could have *money due you from your mortgage escrow account.* More than half the nation's homeowners have these accounts, which are built into their first mortgages (or deeds of trust if they are more common in that part of the country).

This is an amount of money used by lenders to ensure that your property taxes, homeowners insurance and any related expenses are paid on time.

When you make your mortgage payment, you are sending a sum that includes principal and interest on your loan plus the above-mentioned extra amounts set aside for bill payment during the year. Broadly speaking, that is $1/12$ each month added to your mortgage payment.

If a deficiency should arise in your account—due to a tax rise, for example—the lender can ask you to make up that needed amount.

The lender does this to protect its interest in your home, which could be lost in the event of a fire without insurance or through a municipal auction because of unpaid property taxes.

But there are plenty of errors made in this area, mistakes by lending institutions that translate into their holding millions of dollars that rightfully belong to homeowners.

One example: in 1992 the GMAC Mortgage Corp. agreed to settle a lawsuit with 12 state attorneys general who accused the company of overcharging nearly all its 380,000 mortgage customers, requiring them to pay more into escrow accounts than was needed to cover taxes and insurance. The company promised to make refunds but admitted no wrongdoing.

At that time, New York attorney general Robert Abrams, who had helped bring the suit, said 28 million Americans are being overcharged on their escrow payments. Since that time, a few other state attorney general offices have begun looking into escrow overcharges by mortgage lenders.

Here is another story.

A man who asked not to be named said several years ago, when he was three years into owning his home, he received a check for $800 from his lender marked "escrow money." He had not applied for an overage return and says now, with some embarrassment, he also had not checked his mortgage documents to see whether the money was due to come automatically. Even after the windfall arrived, he did not look through his papers for an explanation. It is good news, of course, that he received the $800. But what if he had a different lender? This was obviously money due him, but he had not pursued its return and it could well have sat in his escrow account for years, perhaps never to be returned.

Of course, not all lenders are overcharging. How can you know if *yours* is, and you are due a refund?

Here are some signs that nobody is checking accounts too carefully. Interest rates are going down, but your adjustable rate mortgage payment remains the same, perhaps even rises; a new service company takes over your mortgage and requests more in escrow monies; your lender requests an increase in monthly escrow payments, but you know neither your property taxes nor insurance premiums has risen.

Why does this happen? Sloppy bookkeeping, for the most part. The constant recalculating of adjustable rate mortgages, for example, takes time and offers many opportunities for error.

If you suspect there might be money owed you, you have several ways to proceed. Tying up your money in this manner violates federal law, so you are within your rights to ask that an overage be returned to you.

- If your loan is being held by a financial institution based in your state, call your state banking department or controller's office to see what escrow regulations apply where you live.
- You can ask your lender to allow you to pay those taxes and insurance premiums on your own and not through the institution. Some have policies that allow that; others will respond with a firm no. There are also those who allow those impound accounts to be dropped when the mortgage falls to a certain level.

  Making payments yourself gives you control over where your money goes. Just be certain you will be able to send checks on time. Some homeowners like knowing they do not have to remember when those bills are due and do not have to worry about scraping together sizable chunks of money quarterly for real estate taxes.

  (A note here: Most homeowners with loans insured by the Veterans Administration (VA) or Federal Housing Administration (FHA) and those paying private mortgage insurance are required to have escrow accounts.)
- If you must work through the lender, ask for an accounting of what that institution has been disbursing in your name. Homeowners usually receive statements at the end of the year listing payouts, but if you do not, or if you have trouble understanding cryptic parts of those sheets, by all means give the lender a call.
- You can also learn from your local taxing authority and from your insurance company if you are being charged correctly and

if your bills are being paid when they are due. It happens rarely, but there are some lenders who do not pay those bills on time, incurring late fees that you are paying. Even rarer, fortunately, are those lenders who never make those payments at all!

There is always a chance, when you begin asking questions in this area, you will learn you are paying less than is needed and you will have to make up a deficit.

But of course the reverse could be true too.

If you do not have the time, or, frankly, the inclination, you can hire someone to track down a possible refund for you.

Loantech of Gaithersburg, Maryland (800-888-6781) charges $149 to examine an escrow account. David Ginsburg, Loantech's president, says, "It's really straightforward. You're either right or you're not.

"We've talked to probably thousands of homeowners over the years and 99.5 percent of them do not understand the escrow account. In fact, many lenders don't understand it either. That's probably why there's an error rate there of 50 percent."

Loantech will send you a report on what they have learned about your escrow account and a preprinted form letter you can send to your lender.

Mortgage Monitor (800-283-4887), based in Stamford, Connecticut, will also track your money. Fees start at $219 for a complete audit of either an adjustable-rate mortgage or an escrow account, or $269 for both. The escrow analysis also will let you know if your private mortgage insurance can be cancelled (more about this in the item that follows). You will receive a written report and a customized letter to send to the lender if you have money due you. If there is no response from the lender, Mortgage Monitor steps in to help you secure the money.

"We've got back hundreds of thousands of dollars for people in all 50 states," says Richard Roll, president. Roll noted the monitoring service was able to see as much as $26,000 returned to a single homeowner, monies and interest that had accumulated over 20-plus years.

Private Mortgage Insurance Cancellation

Could you cancel your *private mortgage insurance?* More conveniently known as PMI, these policies allow nearly one-third of the nation's househunters to buy homes with nongovernment mortgages for less than 20 percent down—sometimes as little as 5 percent. They pay a small fee each year for a policy that protects the lender in the event of default.

Did you once buy PMI? Weren't you grateful it was there for you?

But, golly, time passes. For the most part, the policy is supposed to be cancelable when the homeowner's equity has reached 20 percent. But lenders in most states are not required to notify their PMI holders of that fact, so some homeowners are still paying that needless insurance when they have lived in their homes many years and have equity far in excess of 20 percent.

This is a policy offered by a dozen PMI companies nationwide and is not to be confused with homeowners insurance, which is carried by virtually every homeowner for protection in the event of theft, natural disasters, etc.

How much buyers pay for private mortgage insurance depends on the amount of their down payment and the type and term of the loan, plus the type and length of mortgage chosen. You pay less, for example, for a fixed-rate, 15-year mortgage than for adjustable rate mortgages and for 30-year loans.

Rates run about 1 percent of the mortgage up front when the loan is granted and then about 0.5 percent annually thereafter.

You cannot apply to the mortgage insurance company to have your policy canceled. You must make your request in writing to your mortgage lender. You will probably need an appraisal of your home, which you will have to pay out of your own pocket. There may be other conditions, too, one of which will certainly be that you have made your mortgage payments on time over the years you have owned the house.

If you want someone else to do the work for you, you can contact Loantech or Mortgage Monitor (mentioned above). Remember, though, if you think you might have only a few hundred dollars due you, those companies' fees might be a sizable chunk of that sum.

A final point: if you hold an FHA-backed loan, which carries its own form of mortgage insurance, that coverage must be carried for the life of the loan, so you can pretty much dismiss thoughts of cancellation.

But if you have the garden-variety PMI policy, spend a few minutes looking through your mortgage portfolio. You may be able to save a few hundred dollars a year by dropping what might now be needless insurance.

Prepay Your Mortgage

Should you prepay your mortgage? Well, perhaps.

What is involved here is sending your mortgage lender money each month over and above the required loan payment, to be applied to the mortgage *principal*. The object is to pay off the loan sooner, building up equity faster and saving a sizable amount on interest.

You are not *bound* to pay extra money if you want to take this route. It's strictly voluntary, both the amount you send and your stopping the practice if you choose.

You can do this by yourself as easy as pie. Simply attach a note to your monthly payment pointing out to the lender that the check includes *x* dollars that should be put toward principal. Or check off the appropriate box if there is a section for that on your mortgage payment coupon. After you have made the first couple of extra payments, call the lender to be sure they have been entered properly and credited toward the principal. You do *not* want the money applied to your escrow account!

How little can you send? "Pocket change," says Marc Eisenson, publisher of *The Banker's Secret Bulletin*, a financial newsletter. "If you have $10 or $15 a month to spare, add it to your payment."

It adds up. If you have a 30-year, $100,000 mortgage, for example, and pay an extra $25 a month toward the principal, you can save more than $25,000 in interest over the life of the loan. Not planning to stay where you are that long? Then the higher equity you have amassed with extra principal payments gives you that much more for a down payment on the next house. Then you can start making extra payments on *that* mortgage. What we are talking about here, of course, is a system of forced savings.

Can't you just apply for a 15-year loan, you ask? Well, the interest rate you have on your present mortgage might be lower than the prevailing one as you read this. The credit inspection might be closer for the shorter-term loan, and you will be *locked into* those higher payments, where here they are voluntary.

"Prepayment penalties" is probably a phrase familiar to you. It is not practiced much these days, though, so you are not likely to be penalized for trying to cut interest costs on your loan. Penalties are carryovers from the days when there were no, or minimal, fees or closing costs with a mortgage. Today there are closing costs galore to cover, if need be, lenders' losses with prepayments. In the event those penalties still exist with *your* lender, they are likely to be small, perhaps 1 percent of the amount prepaid.

While you can build equity faster with prepaying, there *are* some cautions here.

"If you're carrying credit card debts," says Paul Richard, vice president and director of education for the National Center for Financial Education, a San Diego-based nonprofit organization, "you shouldn't be double-paying your mortgage."

Car loans take precedence too. Indeed, Richard says, any high-interest borrowing should be repaid before you begin adding money to your mortgage payments.

Also, you should obviously not be tossing extra money at your mortgage if your home is, for whatever reason, declining in value. You might also want to investigate whether extra money could be better invested in a mutual fund.

If you would like to work some numbers to see how much you can save, send for *The Banker's Secret* Loan Software, for IBM or Macintosh computers. While the program can help you with virtually any loan (car loans, too), it is especially designed to help with mortgage prepayment figures. The program, which is personalized, comes with a book as well. The price for both is $39.95 plus $3.00 shipping and handling. If you want just the book, *The Banker's Secret*, that's $14.95 plus $3.00. Write Good Advice Press, Box 78, Elizaville, NY 12523, or call 800-255-0899.

Donate Your Home to Charity

This next suggestion can apply to any homeowner, but for the most part it is practiced by those in their sixties, seventies and beyond.

If you have *no* mortgage, you might consider *donating your home to charity*, while continuing to live in it until your death, and receiving a substantial tax deduction now. You reserve "life estate" for yourself.

The value of your gift is determined by a formula that will include your life expectancy and that of anyone else on the deed, using an approved mortality table, and the appraised value of the home.

You can make any specific arrangements you choose with the object of your largesse. "It's all negotiable," says Frank Arnall, a certified financial planner in Orlando, Florida "You might work out a deal where the charity will maintain the house and pay the property taxes. You could be free of those burdens."

Arnall notes that in some cases it might be possible to be paid a small income from the charity, although he qualifies that by adding a reverse mortgage obtained from a lending institution would bring a greater monetary return.

Do you have to have the most splendid mansion in town for a charity to accept your gift? Arnall points out the house's value does not matter. Those who take this step usually have had a favorite charity over the years, and wanting that group to have their home is just a continuation of that support. He recalls working recently with homeowners who had a house valued at $85,000. It was in a neighborhood that had gone up and then down, and the couple was doing some retirement planning that included donating it.

Another couple, he says, cat lovers, planned to leave their house to the local Humane Society. Childless, they have willed a nephew cash and furnishings.

Naturally, this gift will not work for you if you want your heirs to receive your home. If you have none or have provided for them in other ways—over the years, perhaps, or by willing them furnishings, cash and securities—you might want to consider this. As Arnell puts it, "You know that the charity of your choice is getting your home. You get some psychic rewards and some tax deductions, too."

Charge Your Grown Child Room and Board

Do you have a single, adult child living at home who holds a paying job? Are you charging your child for room and board? If you are not and you need the money, consider doing so. Even $15 a week will bring you an extra $60 a month, which can certainly pay a dry cleaning bill and a few other small tabs. Every little bit helps. Those involved in child rearing—parents and professionals—say it is good for the kids, too, to pay "rent," so they will have some idea where money goes and a better concept of the costs of running an apartment or house when they eventually move into their own place. Some parents who do not need that money deposit it in a special account for the child, surprising him or her with a nice check when it comes time to move out.

SUMMING UP

$ If you are willing to work for the money, you might find substantial savings in reading through loan forms, bills and receipts pertaining to your house—and then taking action to secure more favorable terms.

$ Donating your home to a favorite charity can bring tax benefits now and perhaps help with maintenance and real estate taxes.

$ Having working, childless children pay you for room and board is actually doing them a favor, considering all they will learn for the future about budgeting and bills!

INDEX